Chapt 1
Chapt 2 —
3 - .28 - Above Ground
35 - Quote

PICKING UP
THE GUN

PICKING UP THE GUN

A REPORT ON THE BLACK PANTHERS

Earl Anthony

THE DIAL PRESS
NEW YORK, 1970

Library of Congress Catalog Card Number: 70-91118

Printed in the United States of America

Book design by Thomas Clemens

First printing, February, 1970

"If We Must Die" by Claude McKay: Reprinted from *Selected Poems of Claude McKay* by permission of Twayne Publishers, Inc.

To my mother Geraldine
To whom I owe many things.

Author's Note

I decided to join the Black Panther Party, and *pick up the gun,* in April of 1967. That quality in the Party's style and program in those days which completely captured my imagination, and which probably impressed many others in the same way, was a spirit of existential commitment to the goal of revolution.

In one way or another I had been moving, or more accurately, groping toward this objective myself since I had become disenchanted with the course of accommodation so carefully plotted for middle class blacks in America. It was in 1965 that I first became acutely aware of this disenchantment within me and decided I had to do something about it. I went through many personal changes, and became involved in many forms of activity, all toward the goal of the liberation of black people, and thereby liberated this thing which had been gnawing my insides out.

Although now it sounds somewhat naive upon reflection, when I first came into contact with the Black Panthers—with the particularly arrogant way they talked of revolution, their total disdain for the police, and their cold blue steel pistols and rifles—I felt confident that this organization *could* bring about the revolution I had longed for, and more important, bring it about in short order.

I was very impressed, but there was more to it than that; I felt the Party had gone a step further than any other organization in the black liberation movement in America, *and it was a bold step.* It can best be summed up by saying that *the Party had picked up the gun, and dared to put its toe to the line.*

The Party was founded in October 1966, and I was one of the first recruited once it began to expand in the Bay Area to include members other than the handful who started with Huey Newton and Bobby Seale. I was there, witnessed and participated in the growth of the Party from a small, little-known organization with a paramilitary image within the Bay Area to an organization with over forty chapters, two thousand members, and a feared and respected image of military might *vis-à-vis* this nation's police departments and other agencies of the superstructure. Within a two-year period, the Party emerged into the forefront of American radical politics and gained a voice in the international arena as well.

On March 29, 1969, I was expelled from the Party. I was one of those caught in the famous purge of Party members who were counterrevolutionary, adventurists, opportunists, etc. (I don't know what I was.) In February, after two people I worked very closely with in Los Angeles were gunned down allegedly by another black organization the purge started. It lasted three months. Many of the highly involved, top-ranking in the Party were caught in it.

Now that the Party has come into power it is encountering critical problems in maintaining its position. There is internal dissent, attacks and counterattacks between Party leaders and those purged, all of which has surfaced to public attention. In addition testimony before Senate Investigating Committees by ex-Panthers as to dubious activities of the Party, has severely damaged the Party's image. Then there were the alleged assassinations of Party members, who were dissidents and supposed police informers. There have also been defections, the most famous of which were those of James Forman, H. Rap Brown, and Stokely Carmichael.

Along with these internal problems there have been the external forces which have mounted an escalating offensive against the Black Panther Party. The police departments across the nation, in cahoots with the FBI and CIA are on the move to wipe the Party out of existence. Add to this the feuds with other black organizations and you have a situation which is—to say the least—critical for the Party.

None of us, especially those who are black, should forget the contribution which the Black Panther Party has made, and I'm sure is continuing to make, in the struggle for the survival of black people in America. They picked up the gun to show America, so vain and unconcerned in her power over peoples' lives, that when she decided to take another black life she would have to bring ass to get ass. That in itself should be enough to warrant the Black Panther Party the undying respect of black people.

There is another thing which is more important about the Panther experience, to those of us who have no choice but to try and survive and defeat the excesses of America. It has to do with the vital revolutionary process of criticism and self-criticism. We must begin to make a conscious effort not to repeat our mistakes, and the way to do that is to continue to take hard looks at our own experiences. In line with this, we have to take a close look at the bitter feuding within the black liberation movement, and within the Party itself, which has marked the Panthers' rise to power.

Toward this goal of learning by our successes and mistakes, I hope this book makes some contribution. Above all, I have tried to make this account fair.

E. A.

| 1 |

In the summer of 1966 a sixteen-year-old black youth named Matthew Johnson was shot to death in the Hunters Point project in San Francisco. His slayer was a member of the San Francisco police department. Young Matthew was murdered by this cop for allegedly stealing a car. He was unarmed. At the moment that cop shot young Matthew he was judge and jury giving an instant verdict of guilty. There will be no appeals on that case.

This cruel version of law and justice is regularly meted out in the black community. If he had had a chance, young Matthew would have done as well to have decided his fate in the streets of San Francisco by gunfire agains gunfire. *Red Light Justice.*

In 1966 there was a strange mood pervading the black communities across this country. It was that summer that Stokely Carmichael and SNCC had made the cry for Black Power. As Marvin X Jackman, a black San Francisco poet, expressed it: black people were *"sick and tired, and tired of being sick and tired,"* and they were about to do something about their situation. In San Francisco, the murder of young Matthew triggered the anger in the black community, and it exploded as if out of the barrel of a 12 gauge shotgun.

For the next three or four days we followed the pattern that had been set by our black brothers and sisters in Harlem in 1964, Watts (Los Angeles) in 1965, and other black urban areas in America—and surged forward into insurrection—enshrouding black San Francisco in wrath, fire, and bloodshed for two days as stores were looted, warehouses burned, and sniper fire exchanged with the police in Hunters Point and the Fillmore district.

It did not bring young Matthew back—but it did bring into being in San Francisco a revolutionary breed of black men and women. To many—those who had not been in Watts—it was a baptism of fire. An indelible and life-changing experience.

A few days after San Francisco, its sister city across the Bay, Oakland was ignited by insurrection.

When the fall of 1966 set in, there was a new set of dynamics motivating those of us in the San Francisco Bay Area who were actively involved in the black liberation movement. A by-product of the summer's insurrections. People were beginning to group together, to talk about what they could do and make certain efforts to put things in motion. And during this embryonic stage there was mostly talk, as people began to discover that they were black and that there was a distinct problem in this country directly related to their skin color, that people had done things about their problems in other countries, and we should be about examining certain solutions to our problems. It was as the black revolutionary theoretician Frantz Fanon said in his manifesto *The Wretched of the Earth*: "Violence is a cleansing force. It frees the native from his inferiority complex and from his despair and inaction; it makes him fearless and restores his self-respect." It was this type of chemistry—activated by the revolts in the cities—that was operating on people to whatever degree. They were going through changes.

My associates and people that I knew or knew about were reading and quoting Fanon in the fall of 1966. He was to us the apostle of violence. For us *The Wretched of the Earth* was like a road map to revolution, and if you were honest, and intelligent enough not to misinterpret what you had read, you could look on the map and locate the distance you had traveled on the journey. But at the end you knew there was armed struggle. This was the classical way. And this is what we were at *least* talking about in the fall of 1966. But this type of talk was reserved for our most romantic verbal ventures into the hows of solving the problems of black people in America.

In February, 1967, Roy Ballard, the San Francisco SNCC organizer, called a meeting of all of the black organizations in San Francisco–Oakland. Adam Clayton Powell had just been ousted from his Congressional post, and the fourth anniversary of the date when Malcolm X was assassinated was coming up (it always bothers me that we celebrate Malcolm's death rather than his birth) : Ballard planned to use these two pivotal events to pursue that illusive goal—unity among black organizations. After a petition was signed in behalf of Powell, that matter was dropped, and the representatives of the black organizations got down to the business of planning a week long commemoration of the death of Malcolm X.

I was invited to participate in the planning of this affair because at that time I was chairman of a group with the initials I AM, which stood for Independent Action Movement. I AM had been together for six months, and we were mainly involved in organizing a public rent strike, and secondarily in such things as public school boycotts for more black teachers, etc. We, like almost everybody else at that time, had styled ourselves after the SNCC pattern of emphasizing black community organization at every level. Most of us were college students, and within the past couple of years most had left the Movement.

The majority of the people involved in the Malcolm X memorial I met for the first time. Coming from Los Angeles to attend law school in San Francisco I had not had time to cultivate friendships among the black liberation movement set. Since I AM was involved in a rent strike, I was asked to speak during the commemoration under a category loosely entitled *Urban Problems*. There must have been thirty to forty speakers altogether, on every subject you could think of. Among them were Huey Newton, Bobby Seale, Ron Karenga, and Eldridge Cleaver (Karenga was to speak on culture, Newton on politics, Cleaver on prisons). There were also numerous appearances of Afro and jazz combos scheduled, art exhibits, and a fashion show by the Black Student Union at San Francisco State College. Betty Shabazz, the widow of Malcolm X, was to be the keynote speaker on the opening day, and the final event would be a pilgrimage to the death site of Matthew Johnson. For the entire week there would be something going on from 10 A.M. in the morning, to 2 A.M. the next morning.

When the decision came up, as to how the security of Betty Shabazz was to be handled, Roy Ballard suggested that that responsibility be turned over to the Black Panther Party for Self-Defense, a new paramilitary organization that was based in Oakland, and had been founded in October '66 by two Oakland brothers, Huey Newton and Bobby Seale.

At that time, there were many different Black Panther organizations, taking their names and symbolism from the Lowdnes County Freedom Organization that SNCC had played a major role in organizing, and there were two of these Black Panther organizations in the Bay Area: the Oakland based group, the Black Panther Party for Self-Defense, and the San Francisco group which was called the Black Panther Party. There was much debate around that time about the factors that distinguished one from the other. The San Francisco organization, which was headed by Ken Freeman, said that it was political whereas the Oakland group was military (this San Francisco group was to fold shortly after the Malcolm X commemoration). Huey Newton and Bobby Seale, however, said they were *both* political and military.

It seemed that Ken Freeman and Bobby Seale had originally been in RAM (Revolutionary Action Movement) together, but not many people outside the black community of Oakland had heard of Huey Newton, Bobby Seale, and their activities. That was all changed on February 21, 1967. A well-disciplined group of over twenty members of Oakland's Black Panther Party for Self-Defense entered San Francisco's International Airport that day, to escort Betty Shabazz from her plane to an interview at *Ramparts* magazine and on to the Bayview Community Center and her keynote address. The BPPSD was only functioning as a security team that afternoon, but their style and daring caught the eye of the sensation-oriented black liberation movement—and probably more important—that of the white press. Not only was the group that went to the airport well-disciplined, and dressed uniformly in black berets, pants, and jackets, but they were carrying pistols strapped to their sides, 12 gauge shotguns, and carbines. In California in broad daylight at a major airport, and in the midst of thousands of people— mostly white. To most people they were a bunch of "crazy niggers," but whatever people thought, Huey Newton and Bobby Seale were on the scene to stay, and moving toward the center of the stage.

That night Betty Shabazz spoke before an overflowing audience at the Bayview Community Center. In the balconies, serene and aloof, were stationed members of the Black Panther Party for Self-Defense, their guns held expertly but unmenacingly. I remember thinking that all these months we had been talking about Fanon and whether or not to arm ourselves, and here these brothers had picked up the gun. *Everybody had been upstaged.*

Later on that night, after the conclusion of the opening night's events, I searched for more information on the Black Panther Party for Self-Defense. A close friend of mine, Bill Ballon, was the logical person to go to, since he was raised in Berkeley, which borders on Oakland.

Bill related to me what he knew—how Huey Newton and Bobby Seale believed that black people had to be armed, to have a type of military power, because they were powerless in other ways. He told me that Huey and Bobby had hooked up with each other at Merritt College, a junior college in Oakland, where both were members of the Soul Students Advisory Council, that they had armed some young brothers in Oakland.

Shortly after the Malcolm X Commemoration, a place called the Black House became the meeting place of the black nationalist set in San Francisco. There was always something going on there, and people would go around just to hang out. On Friday nights, they began to have meetings open to all black organizations from San Francisco-Oakland. It seemed that a brother named Eldridge Cleaver, who was the founder of the Black House, was pursuing the idea which had been the motive for the Malcolm Commemoration, of uniting all the black organizations in the area into one superstructure.*

One Friday, I went to one of these Black House meetings. A few people in I AM were with me, and we came late. As we walked in, I immediately noticed two young brothers in the far and near corners of the north side of the room, standing at ease with carbines resting snugly in their arms. There must have been twenty to thirty people at the meeting and they were seated in a circle. Many of the faces were familiar ones in the local black nationalist set; among them Barbara Arthur, Roy Ballard, Mark Comfort. At the south side of the room was Eldridge Cleaver who was chairing the meeting. Opposite Cleaver, on the north side of the room, sat Bobby Seale, Huey Newton, and two of their aides, all dressed in black, Huey holding a shotgun, and Bobby with a .45 strapped to his side. The brothers standing as guards were with

---

* I was to find out later that the Commemoration had originally been his idea but he had asked Ballard to execute it because Ballard was better known in the Bay Area.

them. Huey and Bobby seemed aloof from everybody else, but serious and determined.

This meeting was different in some important ways from any black nationalist meetings I had previously attended, and I had attended many in the last year. For one thing, there was none of that circuitous debate over each matter brought to the floor, which had become standard. When Cleaver (who was not officially a Panther, although he definitely played off the Panthers' image that night) put a motion on the floor that the group adopt the BPPSD's Ten Point Program, there was not a word of dissent. This was so unusual for this group that Cleaver commented, rather facetiously, "I know somebody must have something to say?"

Another thing which was different at that meeting was the feeling of revolutionary discipline and commitment. Nobody budged when Cleaver asked anyone who was not serious to leave. I don't believe everybody was serious, or at least serious about *that* meeting, but I also know that nobody wanted all eyes riveted on him as he made what would have been a very long walk to the front door.

Huey, Bobby, and those brothers with guns had really made a difference that night. The whole scene blew my mind. I wanted to find out everything I could about the Black Panther Party for Self-Defense, and about Eldridge Cleaver. By this time it was easy to get information. People in the black nationalist set had begun to nit-pick about the BPPSD and about Cleaver. (This was in early March, 1967, when Cleaver was not yet a member of the Party.) They complained about the aloof and cocky attitude of the BPPSD when they came to Saturday parties at the Black House. They said the group was not political. As for Cleaver, they said he was in love with a white woman, and might be a Communist. The more I heard, the more I became thoroughly convinced that Cleaver and the BPPSD had to be all right, for these particular nationalists only criticized people who were actually doing something, and thereby leaving their company.

A few days after that meeting at the Black House, I was approached by Hank Jones and Chuck Morton, two brothers in I AM, about coming to a meeting they had set up with Cleaver in a small office on Potrero Hill. I jumped at the opportunity.

The purpose of the meeting that night was never really defined. It was more or less to let us feel each other out—to find out what people were moving in what way. A lot of people were going through changes at that time—and there was a lot of probing for direction. That night Cleaver was asked many questions as to what he felt was the direction of the black liberation movement. When I think back to those days, I realize how naive we were to expect pat answers on such historically complex questions. What impressed me about Cleaver was not the solutions he advocated, for he admitted that he was probing like everybody else, but his ability to analyze what pieces it would take to come together to work toward our solution. I had the feeling while listening to Cleaver talk, that this brother was something special, that although he didn't have his thing together yet, he knew what he was about, and was moving to get his thing uptight.

Particularly, I remember Cleaver talking about the need for one unified organization for the black liberation movement in America. He had just returned from a tour with Stokely Carmichael, which he had done for *Ramparts* magazine, and felt that Carmichael had the national image to help bring such a thing about. He also talked about the Bay Area being a political melting pot, and said that it should be the focus for revolutionary activity, black and white, in the country.

For the next week or so after the meeting that night, I did a lot of thinking about the events of the last few months. Unlike any other group, the BPPSD had made a definite impression upon me by the fact that they had picked up the gun and made it the thrust of their program. Also, Cleaver's concept of the direction of the movement had made a profound impression on me. When I heard that he had joined the

Party, it seemed that everything was jelling for the BPPSD.

I decided that it was time to *pick up the gun,* and I searched out Cleaver to find out how to go about joining the Black Panther Party for Self-Defense.

| 2 |

It was in April that I contacted Eldridge Cleaver. We arranged to meet one Sunday at the house of Beverly Axelrod, the San Francisco attorney. The black nationalists who condemned Cleaver at that time for "being in love with a white woman" were referring to his relationship with Miss Axelrod, who had masterminded Cleaver's release from prison. Upon his release, she had introduced him at a party to many of the leaders of the San Francisco black nationalist set, and some of these people were now attacking Cleaver for his affiliation with her.

I came to the home at the prearranged time, the Sunday afternoon of the meeting. The doorbell was answered by a tall, slender, brown skinned brother, with a heavy mustache. He was in shirtsleeves, and tucked into his pants, with only the dark steel of its handle showing, was a .45 caliber pistol. I immediately recognized the brother from the meetings at the Black House—Bobby Seale. Seale didn't know me, and he was very abrupt and businesslike (later I was to find out that this was his way). He told me that Eldridge wasn't in, but I could try again a little later that afternoon. There was no invitation to come in, which seemed to fit neatly into the mental picture I had of the Black Panther Party for Self-Defense being something very serious and clandestine.

When I returned later that afternoon, Cleaver had arrived. He introduced me to five or six Panthers who were also there, and then the two of us went into a room and talked. I told him that I wanted to join the Party. He seemed interested but cautious. I understand why now. At that time the Party membership was small in number, and restricted to the Oakland area. It was beginning to make inroads into the Richmond community through its investigation of the killing of a black youth named Denzil Dowell, by a Contra Costa County sheriff. But the small number of brothers who had been recruited into the Panther Party were almost all off the streets of Oakland and I was one of the first brothers from San Francisco to seek recruitment. Also, I had worked on the planning committee of the Malcolm X memorial with people who were highly critical of Cleaver in particular and the Black Panther Party for Self-Defense in general.

Whatever Cleaver's reservations might have been, he never expressed them verbally—but only left me with the feeling that he was being cautious by the tone of his voice and the line of his questioning. He told me that he had read a position paper on the San Francisco public rent strike that I had done for a Hunters Point community newspaper *The Spokesman,* and he thought my political thinking in that position paper was sound. He asked what year I was in in law school. I told him I was in my final year.

"Good," he said, and then pondered in silence as if quickly fitting that piece of information into a political jigsaw puzzle that he had in his mind, before commenting further. I was to see him do this many times after that afternoon.

"We're going to need black lawyers in the liberation movement," he said next.

Then he went on to explain that he had altered his political direction. That he was no longer trying to form an umbrella organization consisting of different organizations in the area each doing their separate thing, as he had tried to do at the Black House. I sensed that he must have been very disappointed by the futility of his efforts. My own involvement with the various organizations of the Bay Area had driven home the message that we were far from reaching the point where we realized the necessity of joint action. Cleaver explained that from now on he was dedicating himself to the Black Panther Party for Self-Defense, and to building armed defense units in black communities across the country. He told me how he had walked the streets with Huey Newton and Bobby Seale, and that they were doing the best job of organizing he had seen.

I agreed with him. He then took me in to talk to Bobby Seale, the Chairman of the BPPSD, who would make the decision as to whether I would be accepted. Bobby briefly explained what the Party was about, and then told me that they would see how I worked out. At the time I was organizing in the Potrero Hill area of San Francisco, and I was directed to continue my work there but to organize for the Panthers. Aside from that, I was to be left more or less to myself in order to feel things out.

I started trying to catch up with Cleaver in the evenings. If I could, I would go over to Oakland for meetings, or down to North Richmond where the BPPSD was making its greatest organizing push at that time. One Friday night I was told to come to the Black House. There was a social gathering there every Friday night that spring, centering around a poetry reading or dramatic presentation (LeRoi Jones, who was working in San Francisco then, was staging shows and having rehearsals at the Black House); the evenings would be completed by parties. By this time Cleaver was rarely at the Black House, although he was still somewhat loosely associated with it.

As I walked in that night my attention was drawn instantly to two young Panther brothers, in black leather jackets, and black pants, with black berets pulled down on their heads at a slant, each holding a carbine. Whenever I saw the Panthers during those early days with their weapons held expertly and with that confident air that they had, my heart used to skip a few beats. Other people used to tell me they had the same reaction.

It was the first time I had seen the Party at the Friday social, although I was used to seeing them at the Saturday political meetings. The place was packed that evening. People were sitting or standing everywhere. I remember Marvin X Jackman was reading some of his poetry.

Bobby Seale and a couple of his lieutenants were standing toward the rear of the crowd facing Jackman. When I caught Bobby's eye I nodded, and he returned the nod. He had a .45 caliber pistol strapped to his side, and was dressed in uniform. His lieutenants were carrying carbines. When I saw Bobby those first few times, before I really got to know him, he was always grim and determined. Never the faintest evidence of a smile crossing his face. He seemed different from the other black nationalists in the Bay Area that I knew, who always seemed to think they could clown and party their way through the struggle. Once I became involved in the Panthers, I realized how much pressure there must have been on Bobby and Huey in those days.

After the poetry reading, the playwright Ed Bullins announced that Bobby Seale would have a few words to say. The place was already quiet because people had been listening to Jackman, but when Bobby moved to the middle of the floor and began to speak, there was dead silence. Even those in the black nationalist set who were critical of the Party basked in the aura of self-respect and seriousness that the Black Panthers brought to their local efforts.

As I listened to Bobby speak that night, I recalled that when I first saw the Panthers on the scene—armed—I had felt that they had upstaged everybody. But now as the reality of their presence began to painfully expose the truth of what we who believed ourselves committed to the struggle were about—I analyzed their impact upon me and my contemporaries again. This time politically. The Panthers were not content merely to live in the intellectual milieu of black nationalism. Unlike any other organization in the area, they were making a conscious attempt to bridge the gap between their rhetoric and their action.

"We're going down to Richmond tomorrow, where brother Denzil Dowell was murdered by a member of the racist police department. And we're going to be armed. And we're gonna have a righteous rally with the people of Richmond." Bobby's words spurted out as he paced the floor like the graceful jungle cat, the panther.

He asked people to come to the rally. Then he finished his short talk and left immediately with his lieutenants. A certain dullness began to seep into the room. The glow of admiration that had been in the eyes of the black females receded, and was replaced by that stoic stare, the legacy of four hundred years of witnessing the emasculation of black manhood.

I went to Richmond the next day with the Panthers. On the way down I was briefed on the facts in the Dowell case. Denzil Dowell was twenty-two when he was shot to death on April 1 by a white cop from the Contra Costa sheriff's office. Mark Comfort, a black organizer from Oakland who knew the Dowell family, had asked the Black Panther Party to come down and look into the situation. The Panthers went into Richmond and conducted their own investigation, turning up some interesting things—one of these things being that a doctor who had investigated told Dowell's relatives that he had concluded Dowell was shot with his hands raised. He had deduced this from the way the bullets entered the body. Also it became known that Dowell had no gun. Everything pointed to a clear case of unjustifiable homicide.

The Panther Party had taken this information directly to the Richmond District Attorney and the following day had had a meeting with the sheriff of Contra Costa County. At both meetings, which were attended by black people from Richmond, they were armed, and although the agencies of law enforcement were seemingly rigid in their position on the murder, the Party was accomplishing its purpose—the

14 | *Picking Up the Gun*

black community was becoming very interested and involved in the Panther-style investigation.

The people came to the Denzil Dowell rally. Black people, old and young. Not the college students, or the middle class, but the very people who were catching hell every day in that North Richmond community.

The rally was in the yard of George Dowell, Denzil's brother, a Captain in the Black Panther Party. There were several hundred black people there that day. Some sat on the lawn. Others stood and milled around. Standing tall were the Black Panthers, armed, and some of the people from North Richmond had also come with their guns. Bobby Seale and Huey Newton talked to the people. They stood on top of a car, and explained the Panthers' Ten Point Program, and why black people should arm themselves, and how they could put an end to wanton murders like Denzil Dowell's. At one point, Huey, explaining the type of weapons black people should get—pointed to the gun in the hands of a Panther brother on the roof of the house behind him. The brother, a Panther named John Sloan—went through a demonstration of his weapon; the people really dug it.

They dug everything about the Panthers. The way they brashly defied the police verbally (the police watched the rally from a safe distance outside the perimeter of the crowd), the way they openly brandished their weapons. You could see that the Panther Party was establishing a relationship to these people on a very fundamental level. It was the police who had killed Dowell, and who daily intimidated black people in North Richmond—as they did in black communities across the country. And it was the policeman's gun at his side which gave him the ultimate power; the power to take someone's life. But the Panthers were shattering the myth of the omnipotence of the police. (I was later told that on a couple of occasions at an earlier rally in North Richmond, individual policemen had walked toward the area where the people were assembled, but turned away when armed Panthers moved peacefully but determinedly to block their entrance.) By action they were showing what the people already knew, but had never permitted themselves to admit—that the police were just men, but they had guns and the law to back them up. That to counteract this, black people needed to arm themselves, and then find a way of dealing with the police without getting hung up in any legal entanglements.

Everybody seemed to be enjoying themselves. The Panthers were talking the language of the people, and the people were really digging it. Not the people who sip cocktails at fancy parties on top of the hill, upwind from the stench of human suffering and decay below them; but the people who had been washed down into that cesspool which is the collective black historical experience—past and present—in this Babylon called America. When the Panthers said that day that black people should pick up the gun, they understood why.

On the way back to San Francisco that evening I kept replaying the events of the day in my mind. I don't know what I'd been expecting, but I was totally satisfied by what had transpired. I had been involved in the Watts insurrection in 1965, and was in the San Francisco revolt of 1966, but I had never seen black men command the respect of the people the way that Huey Newton and Bobby Seale did that day.

At a later stage of my development in the struggle—when I began to think back on that day in Richmond, as well as the revolts I had been in, and my involvement in the rent strikes—I realized that what seemed so fantastic to me was simply a forward step in ideology and tactics in the continuous process of changing the political, social and economic order of America. But what captured my imagination during my early days in the Party, was *not only* the fact that the Panthers had taken a step forward in ideology and tactics, but the "boldness" of the style with which that step was taken.

The next day which was Sunday April 30, 1967, the *San Francisco Examiner* came out with a front page headline:

Oakland's Black Panthers Wear Guns, Talk Revolution. It carried a picture of Bobby Seale with a .45 caliber pistol strapped across his shoulder, and Huey Newton with a bandolier of bullets across his chest, and a riot shotgun in his hand. The newspaper story detailed some of the more well-known actions of the Black Panther Party, including the Dowell investigation and the armed escort provided Malcolm X's widow, Betty Shabazz, to the Malcolm X Memorial in February. It also talked about the impending gun legislation which was to go before the California Legislature in Sacramento on Tuesday, May 2, 1967.

This proposed legislation, was a thinly disguised attempt to disarm the Panthers. A few weeks before, Don Mulford, an Assemblyman from the Oakland district, had introduced a bill to change the state law which permitted private citizens to carry loaded weapons as long as they were not concealed, and under which permits were required for handguns, but not for rifles or shotguns. This law was the foundation upon which the Black Panther Party was built, and the Oakland police were strongly suspected of instigating the bill to change it.

The day the story in the *Examiner* broke, I was with LeRoi Jones and five or six black nationalist activists. After reading the story, Jones mused over it for a minute, stroking the growth of hair under his chin. "It could be very dangerous. They usually try to set you up this way," he said.

Over the long haul, the wisdom in LeRoi's statement became very evident.

On Tuesday, May 2, I had to answer a subpoena to testify at hearings of the United States Civil Rights Commission in San Francisco. On that same day Huey Newton had dispatched a contingent of twenty-four brothers and six sisters to go to the California State Legislature in Sacramento, where the subject of gun legislation was due on the floor and Mulford was scheduled to speak. Bobby Seale led that delegation. Seale was to read a message to black people—which was sure to get nationwide coverage because of the hordes of media people who were in residence in Sacramento—concerning the necessity to be armed.

It was about five o'clock in the afternoon when I came out of the San Francisco chambers where the civil rights hearings were being held. As I walked out of the Federal Building, a brother I knew as Bo walked quickly up to me, waving a newspaper.

"Dig Earl, Bobby Seale and those crazy-ass niggers have invaded the capitol," he said in a tone which was a mixture of disbelief and agitation.

Sure enough, there it was. In big, bold headlines: *Panthers Invade Capitol; Armed Negroes Invade California Legislature With Guns.* There was a four column picture, right on the front page, of the brothers in their black uniforms, with their weapons held expertly. Even from as cold a form of communication as the newspaper you caught the feeling of the Panthers' confidence—that confidence I had first seen at the Black House—but this wasn't the Black House, this was the capitol building of the largest state in the most powerful country in the world. That picture was worth a thousand words.

"Goddamn, these niggers are a bitch," I said. I was as surprised as anyone, I had not been invited to make the trip, being new to the organization.

It seemed that my chest expanded a few inches, and I held my head a little more erect the rest of that day. I felt justifiably proud not simply because I was a new Panther recruit but because I was a black man.

Within the short span of two weeks in which I had been associated with the Party, my emotional commitment had become deeply entrenched. Later when I became an official in the Panther hierarchy, I used to see that same instant emotional involvement in new recruits—an involvement that progressively deepened. It became common, in fact, to hear Panthers proudly say: "The only way I'm gonna leave the Party will be in a pine box."

| 3 |

Sacramento electrified the nation. What began as a symbolic protest against the gun legislation being introduced into the legislature that day—was turned into a bizarre affair—by the sensationalizing news media—and the bungling law enforcement agencies in Sacramento. The end result was that the white people at the mercy of the news media were led to believe that black men were beginning to march armed on their policy makers—a belief sure to spread a wave of panic in white suburbia. And black people were left confused, however smug they may have felt about the whites' discomfort.

Actually, what had occurred, was that the Party had gone to the State Capitol openly armed, and were met by the media men falling over each other trying to get the best television shots or copy for the late afternoon news. When the delegation led by Bobby (Huey was not there, since he was on parole, stemming from a felony charge he had been convicted of a couple of years prior to his Panther days; if he had made the trip, it would have been grounds to revoke his parole) got to the box reserved for outside observers in the chambers where Mulford's bill was being heard, the confusion which disrupted the hearings was first caused by the mob of newsmen and cameramen. Then the sight of the armed Panthers brought a predictable heightening of the tension, and the guards at the capitol had to assert their authority and begin pushing and shoving news people and Panthers.

No arrests were made on the spot. The Panthers were on their way out of town, making a clean getaway, when they were apprehended by the Sacramento cops while stopping at a gas station. A shoot-out was barely averted by Bobby Seale wisely counseling the brothers to take the "bust." It seemed that the state authorities, knowing that they would be unable to save face if they let those "niggers" come in and pull something that audacious, dragged an old fish and game law out of the books and charged the Panthers with it. Eighteen of the brothers were jailed. Among them were Bobby Seale and Eldridge Cleaver, who was armed with a camera that day, since he came as a reporter for *Ramparts* magazine. All were released a few days later on bail, and six of them later served minor sentences for the Sacramento affair.

Sacramento put the name of the Panthers on the lips of people across the country. However, despite the national publicity, the organization had not solidified its position in its home base of San Francisco-Oakland. Its program was little-known in black communities outside of Oakland and North Richmond, and there was still the disagreement existing among the individuals and organizations in the black nationalist set who had always been at odds with the Panthers for reasons political or personal or both.

Backbiting and petty bickering were very common at that undeveloped stage of the politics of the black liberation movement in the Bay Area. There were at least twenty to thirty splinter groups operating, and each somehow felt that it had the mandate to speak for black people, that it had the correct analysis of the problem which was facing black people in America. In reality, most of these organizations were one-man showcases, and most of the people in the black nationalist set spent their time romanticizing about the revolution we were going to have in America.

Much of this was due to the fact, that although people had developed a high level of political consciousness, and had become totally disenchanted with the conditions of black people in America and the rate of progress that was being made in the black liberation movement, they had not developed the commitment to transform their frustrations and analysis into constructive efforts. Unable to explain their lack of action, they were extremely critical of the Black Panther Party for Self-Defense because the Panthers were making a move to leave the pack, the inner circle, and gain the respect and popularity of the masses of black people.

The friction within the ranks of the black nationalist set in San Francisco-Oakland became more obvious after Sacramento. About this time I began hearing "bad-mouthing" of the Party more frequently. Our enemies constantly attacked us for "not being political." A leader of one faction insidiously said: "They're playing cowboys and Indians."

A few days after Sacramento the Black Panther Party pulled a *coup d'état* at the Black House. Up until the *coup d'état,* the Black House had been under the influence of a particular black nationalist clique in San Francisco, which was cultural in its leanings. This clique was not predisposed to the politics of the Black Panther Party for Self-Defense and had been most critical of the actions of the Party. The Party moved into the Black House armed, and gave eviction notices to members of this clique. They left the premises, and the Black House was then occupied by the Black Panther Party for Self-Defense.

Since the Black House had been the center of non-Establishment culture in San Francisco, and the meeting place for most members of the black nationalist set, its take-over was an omen of things to come. The black nationalists with cultural leanings were probably the strongest faction opposing the Party. When the Party moved into the Black

House, and set up base, it was the beginning of its move to abolish the factionalism which was plaguing the black liberation movement in the Bay Area.

At the same time that the Party was developing in Oakland, there was the San Francisco-based Black Panther Party. There had always been bitter dissension between the two organizations over the correct revolutionary ideology. The San Francisco organization said that they were political, and that the Oakland organization was paramilitary, and their position was that the political struggle must be waged first. Huey and Bobby, from the beginning, stated that the Party was a political party, and that political power for black people in America lay in being able to deal a political consequence—which for us was through military power. The Black Panther Party for Self-Defense would retort to critics who said that it was not political the words of Chairman Mao Tse-tung of China: "Political power grows out of the barrel of a gun."

After Sacramento the similarity between the two names caused a great deal of confusion. People would come looking for the Panther Party that had gone armed to the state capitol, and mistakenly end up in the clutches of the San Francisco organization, which would go to great lengths to explain the difference between the two organizations and create further confusion.

A delegation of Black Panther Party for Self-Defense members went to a fund-raising party given by the San Francisco Black Panther Party. There was a discussion between officials of the San Francisco group and the delegation from the BPPSD about the possibility of either a merger or the San Francisco organization giving way to the popular will of the people—who recognized the Oakland organization—and changing its name.

The San Francisco Panthers were obstinate and refused both proposals. There were heated words and gunshots were fired into the floor and ceiling as the verbal negotiations broke down. People fled the party, and the meeting between both organizations ended on that sour note.

The San Francisco Panthers accused the Oakland Panthers of provoking an attack upon them. Two days after the incident they went *en masse* to the main office of *Ramparts* magazine, where Eldridge Cleaver, who had become Minister of Information, worked as a staff writer, and they picketed (the factionalists were particularly against Cleaver, who had pushed for a united organization ever since he had come on the scene). They carried signs which said: *Ramparts Supports the Black Panther Party for Self-Defense;* and *The Black Panther Party for Self-Defense Is Communist Backed.*

Less than a month after the picketing demonstration outside of *Ramparts,* the San Francisco-based Black Panther Party faded from the scene of their own accord. Most of the other factionalist elements also disappeared into the woodwork. This was the result of the increased conflict and tension that had surfaced in the Bay Area. The pressure had become too great to bear.

I was made Captain of the San Francisco area. This was right after Sacramento, when the Party had come to a rally that I had set up in the Potrero Hill area. The rally was successful, and my appointment followed immediately. A Captain within the Party is the highest position of the rank and file. He is the direct link between the rank and file and the officials of the ministries. He is the man in the middle, and it is probably the toughest position in the Party (the position became increasingly tough when the organization became national; sometimes I feel I was fortunate to be a member of the ministry in the early days with a different set of responsibilities) .

The political organizing of the Party within the black communities in Northern California was escalated after Sacramento. We began to go into black communities that we had not touched before, and to have rallies with the people. The thrust of this organizing was to educate black people in these communities as to the power they would possess, and the legitimate threat they would become to the police, which was the first line of defense for the power structure, if they were armed. On a pragmatic level, the Party would form ca-dres of young blacks from the communities, initially re-cruiting at the rallies themselves. We knew the importance of having black people sympathetic to our political views, for the people are always the life line of any revolutionary party. We also understood the importance of having cadres from the revolutionary party live in the communities within which they would work.

As we were escalating our political work, the police be-gan escalating their repression. The police authorities had comprehensive intelligence reports on the Party. They had pictures of most of the members, and the license numbers of the cars we drove. When the Panthers gained public notori-ety, the police stepped up the pressure and arrested Panthers under any pretext.

Huey was jailed for profane language and for carrying a knife with a blade which was long enough to be considered dangerous. Bobby Seale and Little Bobby Hutton were ar-rested for entering a courthouse with loaded weapons. A pat-tern was developing; the police authorities were provoked by the widespread acknowledgment of our political views, and we felt that they would use any pretext to draw Party mem-bers into a gun battle, where they could justifiably kill key members. It was only logical now that we should make the decision to cease publicly carrying guns. Suicide was not what the Party was about.

We began to focus the main thrust of our efforts on our newspaper: *The Black Panther Community News Service*. I remember we used to work on the newspaper at Eldridge's apartment. We had set up a drawing board there, and had two or three typewriters scattered around the room. There were usually six or seven of us in the room, stepping around each other, as we rushed to bring out a weekly edition. We did all the work ourselves, and were working with the most modest equipment. (Bobby Seale would do the layouts, fas-tidiously determining where each article and essay would be placed on the page, the position of the art and photos. After

Bobby laid the paper out, Eldridge would discuss the material that would go into it with the rest of us. We would write and type the whole thing right there in the apartment. It was our city room.) In the newspaper we began to refer to the police as "pigs." We were looking for the most despicable name to call the police, and the pig is symbolically the nastiest animal. "Pig" caught on very naturally, and became a byword used by black people and white radicals. (Later, on television programs about radical movements I was often to hear the word "pig"—a symbol of success in America, to have television use your symbols.)

The newspaper was very blunt. If it was decided that a person was an enemy of the people, we would not hesitate to attack. In one of our early issues, we had a "bootlickers gallery," where there were pictures of Martin Luther King, Jr., Senator Edward Brooke, Floyd McKissick, Whitney Young, James Baldwin, Bayard Rustin and Roy Wilkins. People were shocked that the Panthers would put Rustin and McKissick in the same class as Wilkins and Young. What was probably bothering them was that the Party not only attacked obvious enemies, but was unceremoniously attacking popular and respected leaders of the Movement, past and present. Many people were concerned because they feared that they might be the next to feel the wrath of the Panther attack.

For the next three or four months in the spring and summer of 1967, we were constantly together—at Eldridge's apartment—putting out the newspaper—then going into the streets to sell it ourselves. In between work on the newspaper, we would organize in the black communities around the San Francisco-Oakland area, holding street rallies.

I really began to know Huey Newton during this period. There was a deep respect for Huey among the Panthers at that time, and when he was later imprisoned, this respect became something which was almost sacred. Huey had founded the Party with Bobby Seale. But even Bobby acknowledged Huey's role as the person who put the program together, who went into the streets and armed a handful of young black brothers, trained them in the political writings of such revolutionaries as Mao Tse-tung, and put them back onto the streets of Oakland in armed patrols watching out for high-handed police tactics in the black community.

Huey was the soul of the Black Panther Party. When the Party became a national organization, which was after Huey was in jail, the few brothers still around who could make the statement, "I walked with Huey," were held in high esteem within the ranks of the Party. It was a point of historical reference in the Party's growth, and showed that you had come through the tough days of the armed patrols (the patrols were ended after Sacramento—they were to return later—but never were armed openly again) before it was prestigious to be known as a Panther.

The tactic of carrying guns openly in the streets was the thing that people pounced upon most often to attack the Party. Critics would contend that this made the Panther Party too visible a target. There was a severe paranoia around that time in the black liberation movement. Everybody thought their phones were tapped, that every room they went into was bugged—with the police and FBI lurking around every corner to kill them or imprison them on some bogus charge.

This paranoia determined the *modus operandi* of the most serious organizations in the black liberation movement. They carried on their revolutionary activity underground in order to elude the grasp of the law enforcement agencies. The problem with most of these underground organizations, however, was that the FBI and police were underground with them. When they surfaced to perform some revolutionary act, it was usually a setup, and the members of the organization were "busted" attempting to pull off the revolutionary act. The act was never accomplished, and the masses of black people were in the dark as to what the whole thing was about.

In 1965 there was the abortive attempt to blow up the

Statue of Liberty. And in the summer of 1967, there was the conspiracy to kill Roy Wilkins, Whitney Young, and other civil rights leaders of that caliber. Seventeen brothers were arrested for that. Also, there was a so-called plot to poison the water and food supply of the Philadelphia police. Many very serious brothers were arrested. What these incidents had in common was the haze of confusion which surrounded them.

It was common for the Panthers to be attacked by the intellectual element of the black liberation movement. One day Huey received a letter from a brother who had been a member of the New York Black Panther Party (this Panther Party had no affiliation with our organization; later we were to establish a New York Chapter, but this was long after the original New York Panthers had folded). The letter was a mixture of a direct attack on the New York Panthers and other supposedly underground organizations, and an indirect attack on our organization, by its implication that we might be the victims of the same ills. We were on our way across the Bay Bridge going to a rally in San Francisco when Huey read the letter to me. The brother accused the New York Panthers of talking about armed revolution and then being afraid to go into the bars of Harlem and organize the people they were talking about arming. The gist of his argument was that organizations with a political line that put them into a paramilitary stance were more bluff than anything else. Huey was furious. He did not take lightly the program of the Black Panther Party, or the business of revolution. He began to define to me the differences between the Black Panther Party and the other organizations that typed themselves as revolutionary. (Some of the points he made that day were later incorporated into what I considered his best essay: "The Correct Handling of a Revolution.") Huey explained that he first armed brothers publicly as a way of educating black people by example that they must arm themselves against the oppressor. This far outweighed the tactical disadvantage of making the Party a visible target. Huey criticized revolutionaries who were in fact afraid to openly and physically resist the power structure and therefore remained incognito.

According to Huey's concept, the vanguard—which he considered the Black Panther Party—would first be above ground. Eventually it would be driven underground to wage the armed struggle, but by then the masses would seek it out. When it had gathered enough strength, the vanguard would emerge openly again to lead the people to victory.

I must honestly say that at that time I thought Huey had read too much Fidel Castro and Che Guevara. But I was missing the point. There are certain basic principles which are applicable to all revolutions, and a revolutionary leader of his people, if he is serious, must formulate a program right through to the end. Huey was completely serious and he had tried to do this. This is what was important. He was ready to argue his program for the liberation of black people in America to the end.

In his testimony at his trial after the abortive attack on Fort Moncado in Cuba, Fidel Castro used the occasion as a political forum to tell the Cuban masses his program for revolution—he did not try to cop out in any way in the statement of his defense. It was this type of revolutionary commitment that I saw in Huey Newton when he would painfully explain his program, and the necessity of doing things which might be considered mistakes in the present, but which he felt would be proven correct when they became part of the historical legacy of the black liberation movement.

A question which was constantly raised in the circles of the black liberation movement was how we were going to wage guerrilla warfare inside America. What made this impossible, certain people reasoned, was the fact that we did not have any mountains to retreat to like Castro had, for instance, in Cuba. The answer to the question was right under our noses. The guerrilla camps in the urban areas of North America were the apartments in the ghettos of the black community.

We had to use our terrain to the best advantage. The black communities were compact and cordoned off, and guerrilla bands could operate there within a sympathetic political climate.

In the next few months as small groups of us were spending so much time together and doing our political work in one or two apartments situated right in the black community, I began to see how a guerrilla struggle might function. An apartment was far more anonymous than a dingy store front office which is an open target for the police. In the apartment, behind the locked door, with an apartment number, like any other apartment number in the black ghetto, you can do some heavy plotting against the enemy. If everybody in the black community, or a large majority, were politicized to the level that they were armed and regarded the police as the enemy, the police would not go rushing in kicking down doors in the black community, for fear of getting their legs shot off.

The Black Panther Party was like a small community within a community. It was common to see five or six brothers in the Party living together. One brother would get an apartment, because he had a job or access to the apartment for whatever reason, and five or six brothers would move in with him. Constantly being around one another, eating, sleeping, and working together helped to psychologically sustain these brothers and keep them on their toes about their political and military work.

You have to be clever to stay ahead of the enemy in the black liberation movement. The problems of finding money, transportation, and a place to rest your head are all part of surviving. I found out—as did many other brothers—that the best way was to find a black sister who was also involved in the struggle or sympathetic—and you two could share the responsibility of the work of the black liberation movement. If you were involved completely in political work, she could work a job to take care of the practical necessities.

One evening that summer of 1967—I believe it was in June—I rode to San Francisco International Airport with Eldridge. He told me he was going to pick up his "righteous woman," who was coming in from Nashville, Tennessee. We picked up three people at the Airport that night—Fred Brooks, a heavy-set brother, who was then Director of the Nashville office for SNCC; a Caucasian fellow, whose name I don't remember now; and then there was this sister, Kathleen Neal, who was tall, slender, and light complexioned, with a big, red, African bush hairstyle. Kathleen was then with SNCC in the south, working as a program secretary for the campus program; it was she whom Eldridge referred to as his "righteous woman."

Fred Brooks and the Caucasian fellow stayed only a few days. Kathleen Neal had come to stay for good—and she was to become an integral part of the Party operation. Eldridge had met her a couple of months before at a student conference given at Fisk University in Tennessee, when he was traveling and writing a story for *Ramparts* magazine on Stokely Carmichael. She later married Eldridge—and became Kathleen Cleaver.

I had my first direct contact as a Panther with the police on July 23, 1967. Now the contacts between black people and police are usually abrasive and hostile, but add to this the factor that the black person is a Black Panther, and you have a situation so tense and explosive that any questionable move or verbal exchange may precipitate a shoot-out, the police usually being the aggressor.

We were on our way to Los Angeles from San Francisco; Bobby Hutton, Reggie Fortier, and myself. A couple of days before, Bobby and Reggie had been involved in a fight on the campus of Merritt College, along with Huey and Bobby Seale, with some white racist members of the American Nazi Party. Huey said something from the audience at the outdoor rally given by the Soul Students Advisory Council, and one of these helmet-wearing, crazy-ass white boys jumped on his back. Bobby Seale, Little Bobby, Reggie, and another brother commenced to whip the white boy and his partners who came to his aid. I was going to Los Angeles to see about my draft status—and it was decided that Little Bobby and Reggie should lay down there with me until things cooled off, because the incident had received extensive coverage on the local news media, and the police would use any flimflam reason to arrest them since they were known Party members.

Little Bobby was the first young brother off the block to be recruited by Huey and Bobby Seale into the Party. He was sixteen then, and had worked in 1966 on a summer poverty program job where Bobby Seale had been his counselor. Little Bobby was the treasurer of the Party, and was about 5 feet 7 inches tall, and slight, which was the reason for his nickname (in a picture in the newspaper after Sacramento, you see Little Bobby standing tall next to Chairman Bobby Seale, with a shotgun which was almost as big as he was, and wearing that hat that he always wore, cocked to the side of his head). He was always around with Huey, or Bobby Seale.

Reggie was also one of the Panthers who had been at Sacramento. He and his brother Sherwin were among those who could say *I walked with Huey*. Reggie was about twenty-one, and took the program of the Panthers very seriously. Later, in December 1968, Reggie was arrested for attempted murder in a shoot-out with the police in San Francisco.

Little Bobby, Reggie, and I had almost completed our trip; we were coming into Los Angeles when a motorcycle cop flashed his bike light on us, and signaled for us to pull off the freeway. It was a bad time for an interruption, because we had just lit up a joint. When we pulled off the freeway, I quickly got out from under the driver's wheel and went back to where the white cop was, trying to stall for time while Reggie was supposedly getting rid of the marijuana.

After searching me for weapons, the cop made me open the trunk of the car. When he saw a stack of Black Panther papers, he became so tense and ecstatically excited, that I thought he was going to reach a climax right there in the streets. He closed the trunk, and ordered me to put my hands, extended, on the trunk. Then going around to the curb side of the car, he unhooked the strap to his holster and cocked the hammer on his service revolver.

He ordered Bobby and Reggie to get out of the car. They hesitated for what seemed like the longest minute I have ever experienced. Finally, Bobby climbed out from the back seat, and following the order of the cop put his hands on the top of the car. Reggie still remained inside. The cop ordered Reggie to get out twice more, and was obviously getting very nervous as he drew his service revolver halfway out of the holster. Finally Reggie stepped out. I had wondered why he was taking so long, knowing that he wasn't armed; but when he came out I realized why. Reggie still had the package with the three reefers in it (I asked Reggie later in jail why he had not eaten the reefers, and he told me that he figured we needed them with the weekend upon us).

When the cop wasn't looking Reggie let the cigarette package drop to the ground. But then the cop accidentally stepped on it. He really was overwhelmed then. He called on his bike radio, saying that he had three Black Panthers, and something about the reefers. It wasn't five minutes later before there were ten cop cars at the scene. You would have thought the charge was bank robbery, instead of suspicion on possession of marijuana. We were pushed into a police car, and taken to Central Booking in Los Angeles.

They cut Bobby loose after questioning. The police often do that, hoping to arouse suspicion in the other crime partners that the person who has been cut loose has "given them up." Reggie and I knew better about Bobby. The police kept asking us questions about the Black Panther Party. They had confiscated the newspapers, and they were sitting around the room where we were held before going to jail, reading the paper and smugly laughing at the references to "pig" cops (I asked one cop why didn't he pay for the paper he had; he told me where I was going I wouldn't need the money). They got a big kick out of the whole thing.

32 | *Picking Up the Gun*

We were jailed, and about a week later released on bail. We later beat the case because of illegal search and seizure.

The summer of 1967 signaled the end of an important chapter in the black liberation movement. This era, which began with Harlem in 1964, and reached its peak with Detroit in the summer of 1967, will probably be recorded as the insurrectional stage of the black liberation movement. Although there were insurrections in the cities after Detroit (mainly those after Dr. Martin Luther King, Jr.'s death in April 1968)—for the most part, black people have had no taste for Pyrrhic victories since.

But 1967 was a hot summer. This Babylon called America was on fire. Newark was on fire. Milwaukee was on fire, Detroit was on fire. San Francisco, which had experienced insurrection the summer before, did not escape this madness which was raging across the country. After Detroit, for a few days, there was sporadic looting and burning in San Francisco.

About six or seven of us had a meeting in San Francisco, where it was decided that we should protect ourselves in case the insurrection really became infectious in San Francisco and Oakland. We knew the police would attack us first; they could justify their actions because of the public image of the Party as a gun carrying, violent group of black men. It would make no difference to them that the Party had stated that it did not believe in insurrection as a revolutionary tactic.

That night we attempted to gather the proper weapons. Among the six or seven of us, we could only muster three carbines. Most of the Panther weapons had been confiscated in Sacramento and in subsequent arrests, and the police authorities were holding them for evidence. Fortunately, things calmed down.

Bobby Seale went to Santa Rita County prison in August, 1967, to serve a sentence for the Sacramento incident (he served six months, on a misdemeanor charge). After Sacramento, the Establishment in California had succeeded in dissipating the strength of the Party by arrests, bail, and constant pressure. That is how they work—not to destroy you overnight, but by the process of attrition.

The Party was at a very low ebb, but Eldridge was a strong brother. He kept faith. He told me during that time: "The Party is going to take over California in 1968." Only a man with vision would make such a statement during the crisis period we were enduring as the fall of 1967 set in.

I will never forget the night of October 26. Huey, Eldridge, and myself were sitting in Eldridge's apartment. We were talking about many things. What stuck in my mind was a discussion of Thomas Wolfe's *Look Homeward Angel*. Huey was talking about the significance of a passage, where Wolfe talks about crossing the river and getting to the other side, and never being able to go back. He saw a parallel in starting to fight for your liberation as a black man and never being able to submit again.

That night Huey and I went over to a place where James Baldwin was staying at the time and gave him some Black Panther papers for his information. Then we went across the Bay to Oakland and stopped in a few night clubs. Huey brought me back across the Bay, and left me at the Half Note, a night club on Divisadero Street in San Francisco. It was the last time I was to see Huey free, not caged like an animal.

It was about four in the morning of October 28, 1967, that I heard the newscast on a black soul music station. It said that Black Panther founder Huey P. Newton had been seriously wounded in an early morning gun battle in Oakland with two policemen. One policeman, John Frey, was dead. Another policeman, Herbert Heanes, was seriously wounded.

I was mentally paralyzed with shock. I did not want to trust my ears, and although I knew I'd heard it, I felt that I had to confirm it. After I began to emerge from my shock, I hoped desperately that Huey was okay. I cursed the lousy

Oakland police, for I knew that they were down wrong, and had tried to set up brother Huey.

I felt rage. I remember a line from James Baldwin which best describes my feeling that day: "To be black and conscious in America, is to be in a constant state of rage."

This rage is what makes whatever Huey Newton did that morning of October 28 acceptable to me, and whatever Frey and Heanes did unacceptable.

| 4 |

The wounding of Huey that night was a paralyzing blow to the Party. Huey was our comrade, and most important, he was the leader. He had started the Party in October 1966, and now, only a year later, he had staggered into Kaiser Hospital in Oakland, with a bullet hole in his stomach. (Hospitals report all cases of bullet wounds; and when Huey got to Kaiser, they reported it. The police immediately arrived on the scene, and upon recognizing Huey, handcuffed him to the operating table before they would let the doctors take out the bullet. It was the beginning of the changes that he was to be put through in hospitals.)

In Huey's wake at 7th Street and Willowbrook in the heart of the Oakland black ghetto, where pimps, prostitutes, hustlers, and junkies hang out, lay two white policemen. John Frey was dead. Herbert Heanes was seriously wounded. As hard as we tried to be optimistic, the future for Huey looked dismal. During those first few days after the shooting, we were faced with the knowledge that even if Huey survived his wounds, the gas chamber loomed in his future.

The same day Huey was wounded, there was a black arts festival in Hunters Point, the black ghetto where the San Francisco revolt started in 1966. When the young black brothers and sisters began assembling that afternoon they talked about nothing but Huey. They had read about it, for it was on the front page of all the daily newspapers in San Francisco and Oakland (one newspaper carried the trademark photo of the Party—Huey in the African wicker chair, a rifle in one hand, a spear in the other hand, in full Panther uniform), or they had seen or heard reports of the shooting on television or radio.

It was clear to them that Huey was right, and Frey and Heanes were in the wrong. Most of them knew very well that the police will not hesitate to take your life. Matthew Johnson, the young martyr of the Hunters Point revolt, had been only one of many young blacks shot to death by the police.

Huey had instantly become a hero to these young blacks. You could feel it that afternoon in Hunters Point. Huey had talked about the police being an occupation army within the black community. He had said that black people should arm themselves against wanton police brutality and murder. And Huey had not only armed himself and other Black Panthers —he had put his words into action. He went into the streets to contest the evils of the police, and the young black brothers and sisters felt that the police had tried to murder Huey that morning for doing just that.

Less than a week later three policemen were shot while riding in their squad car in Hunters Point. One of them later died. The *Sun-Reporter,* a weekly black newspaper in San Francisco, reported that police authorities felt it was a Panther retaliation. The Party had time and again stressed that the police were the enemy, and that you don't get your revenge for police brutality and murder by rioting in the streets as we had done when Matthew Johnson was killed, but you attack the enemy by using guerrilla tactics—sniper attacks, or police station bombings. Although the Party did not execute that attack in Hunters Point, the young black brothers were beginning to accept the leadership of Huey and the Party, and the attack was done Panther style.

The Panther newspaper that week carried a drawing by

our revolutionary artist Emory, with pictures of Heanes, Frey and the three cops shot in Hunters Point. A caption with the drawing said that *"three little piggies got away"*— referring to the three of the five cops who had survived in the gun battles during that week.

That edition of the Black Panther paper must have started many cops thinking about their personal well-being. A black policeman, who worked his beat in Potrero Hill, a black community in San Francisco, wrote a letter to the Party asking that we spare his life. He told us about his family, and asked us to believe that he wasn't one of the black cops who whip black brothers and sisters with more enthusiasm than their white counterparts.

I have to admit that he was a very smart black cop. He was trying to make sure that he was recognized as a brother just trying to work and make some money, and not an enemy of the people (although the final judges of that are the young black brothers and sisters that he was dealing with day after day). I guess he knew that when he was out there on that beat he was by himself.

The Saturday morning that Huey was shot, Eldridge Cleaver swung into action very quickly. At that time the Panther central staff was Bobby Seale as Chairman, Huey Newton as Minister of Defense, and Eldridge Cleaver as Minister of Information. With Huey wounded in the hospital, and Bobby in Santa Rita prison, the reins of leadership of the Party fell into Eldridge's hands.

Eldridge regrouped the few of us who were left—in what could loosely be called the backup leadership to Huey and Bobby, and we began to take care of the immediate tasks at hand—the humble beginnings of what became the sustained struggle to save the life of Huey Newton, and to popularize his ideas and example to the masses of black people, and progressive white people in America and around the world.

The hard core of the Panthers probably consisted of about fifteen brothers. Most of these were very young brothers, and although none of them lacked determination their skills were not of the type most needed at that time in building a defense for Huey. It was necessary for us to build a machinery that would function effectively in Huey's defense. There were certain adjustments in our program that we were going to have to make as they became necessary, because of the situation.

A sister named Barbara gave us the use of her San Francisco apartment as headquarters for the Free Huey Movement. We also were given the apartment of a sincere young black school teacher, Weldon Stroud (Stroud later lost his job in the San Francisco school system—in reprisal for his public support of the Panther program). With the use of these two apartments, we had established a physical base, and we began to contact people around the country explaining the week by week progress of Huey, and our efforts to free our comrade. Also, we began to produce thousands of written words about Huey and the program of the Panthers for which he was largely responsible.

Huey stayed only a few days in Kaiser hospital, and then he was charged with murder in the first degree, attempted murder, and kidnapping. The kidnapping charge came about because Huey was driven to Kaiser by a black man. He and Gene McKinney, who was with Huey that night, came upon this black man a few blocks from the scene of the shooting, and asked him to drive Huey to the hospital. The State of California said that the driver was asked at gunpoint.

They sent Huey from Kaiser to the hospital ward at San Quentin prison. In the prison setting, where the power of the Establishment is naked and overt and there is little necessity to mask your feelings, the police authorities began to vent their hatred upon Huey.

At first, no visitors were allowed to see him. Then Eldridge contacted Beverly Axelrod, the attorney who had always responded when needed, and she got a court order allowing her to see Huey as his attorney.

I honestly feel that they would have killed Huey in the

prison hospital if contact could not have been established with the outside world. The prison guards in the hospital were really beginning to freak out in their ways of torturing our brother and setting him up so that they could justifiably murder him. The stories of their escapades began to leak out to us.

Because of his abdominal wounds, tubes had been placed in his abdomen as a part of his medical treatment. The pig cops would kick his bed, loosening the tubes in his abdomen, and making Huey suffer in agony. A jive nigger bitch, who was supposed to be a nurse, lied to Huey about helping to devise a way for him to escape from the prison hospital ward. She promised to steal a shotgun and place it in his room. Huey must have felt desperate around that time, but he did not lose his composure and fall for that weak game.

These reports began to filter into the black community, and there settled in the minds and hearts of the Panther Party members a resolve that we were not going to let anybody, no matter what power they seemed to possess, kill our comrade, brother, and leader—Huey Peter Newton.

The reports of the treatment of Huey had snapped us out of the sleepwalking trance that we had been in the first few days after the attempt had been made on his life. We pulled ourselves up by the bootstraps and launched an offensive. The following ultimatum was sent out: *If You So Much As Touch A Hair On Huey's Head, You Better Give Your Soul To God, Because Your Ass Belongs To The Black Panther Party*. It was first given in an editorial in the Panther newspaper, in early November. The Party had sounded the battle cry.

As I have said, the reins of leadership had fallen into Eldridge's hands, and what he did with that leadership during this crisis period was outstanding. Eldridge had previously stayed in the background when Huey and Bobby were operating on the scene, making suggestions that were followed most times because of the high esteem in which this brother was held. He had unselfishly accepted the leadership of Huey and Bobby because of the personal trust he obviously had in these brothers, although at times it seemed that he should have asserted himself more. But whatever personal attributes he had, he seemed always to be able to submit himself to the leadership of the Party.

Another obvious reason that Eldridge had stayed in the background was his parole status. He had been released from the penitentiary in December 1966, after serving nine years of a fourteen-year sentence. Being on parole is like being in prison out of prison, for the parole authorities still dictate what you can and cannot do

As soon as brother Eldridge's feet touched ground in December 1966, he had started out in political work. In April 1967, he made a speech at Kezar stadium in San Francisco, at a rally against America's intervention in Vietnam. The California Adult Authority warned him against making any further political statements that were unfavorable to the federal or state government. When Eldridge went to Sacramento with the Party and was arrested, the Adult Authority were inexhaustible in their attempts to find a charge against him that would put him back into the joint for the remaining four and a half years of his sentence. But Eldridge had outsmarted them—he had gotten clearance from his local parole board to go to Sacramento as a reporter for *Ramparts* magazine. Up until Huey was shot, Eldridge had even gone so far as to sign his uncompromising attacks against the Establishment in the Panther newspaper, *Minister of Information, Underground,* rather than using his own name. But now Eldridge stepped forward to personally shape the destiny of the movement for the defense of Huey.

Once he told me why he felt it was so important that Huey's life be protected at whatever cost. Huey was worth saving as an individual. As Eldridge said: "He was more serious than we were at that time; and we had to get to where he was." I don't know whether Eldridge was completely serious with me; because if he was, he had pulled even with Huey without even realizing it.

Huey's personal well-being was uppermost in the minds of fellow Panthers, but what we were striving to make his defense exemplify to outsiders was a landmark in the history of black people—a showdown with the racist forces of America who had killed countless black leaders or incarcerated them or made them fugitives when they had become too dangerous.

Less than a week after the shooting, we organized a meeting with individuals and organizations in the black liberation movement for the purpose of establishing a Huey Newton Defense Fund.

The meeting was well attended by over a hundred black brothers and sisters—some representing organizations, most just representing themselves. To have that many of us in the same room is rare. It only happens when there is a crisis. If there is no crisis, it is impossible to bring even two representatives from different organizations together to talk about anything, no less to work together. (The squabbling and bickering, petty jealousies and power plays between black organizations is the curse of the struggle. Then to compound things you have factions within organizations, always at each others' throats. You can never be sure who is behind your back.)

I saw people at that meeting whom I had not seen since the Party pulled its *coup d'état* at the Black House six months earlier. In fact, the meeting was composed mostly of those black nationalists whom the Party branded as cultural nationalists. Sometimes I wonder whether they came back then because the defense of Huey's life was a noble cause, or because the emotional atmosphere around them dictated that at least a token effort be made.

Many people present were familiar faces on the black liberation movement scene at that time: Jimmy Garrett of the BSU of San Francisco State (vanguard of the black student movement in America); Bill Bradley, of the Afro-American Institute; Roland Snellings, the writer; and Abdul Karim, editor of *Black Dialogue* (I lived with this brother for a period, and thought highly of him as a person); among others.

We formed an elaborate network of committees. There was a steering committee, publicity committee, finance committee, etc. I believe we had ten in all. We wanted to let everybody get into the act for we knew that if we excluded anybody who considered himself important it would be a blow to his ego, and he might start bad-mouthing the Defense Fund before it got started. A brother by the name of Jim Lacey, who had just returned from Africa, was elected Chairman of the Huey Newton Defense Fund.

The Party members purposely stayed in the background, for we wanted the Fund to visibly demonstrate unity among black organizations in support of Huey. We also realized that black people who were not involved in the black liberation movement might not particularly relate to the Party, because of the image projected by us of being the first organization after the cry for Black Power to pick up the gun; but we hoped to relate to them on the level of justice for an individual black man—Huey Newton—and publically divorce our politics from our defense work as much as possible.

The life span of the first Huey Newton Defense Fund was less than a month. The committees we set up never functioned correctly. The publicity committee, for example, was composed of five or six active black writers, who did not write a solitary word during this first month. This was because there was a head-on clash between Eldridge and a few members of the committee, people who might be branded as cultural nationalists (although I think that this fashion of typing people, *i.e.*, cultural nationalists, etc., has been stretched way out of proportion). One of Eldridge's antagonists said that his life had been threatened by the Party, and this created critical divisions within this initial Defense Fund. The wounds inflicted by the prior disagreements between the Panthers and other organizations had not healed, and the renewed contact had only served to reopen these wounds.

Meanwhile, individuals who were not involved in the black liberation movement in an active way began to come forth in support of Huey. Fund raising benefits were given almost every night somewhere in the Bay Area in that first month or so. Churches began to take up collections for Huey at their Sunday services. Telegrams and letters of support flowed in from around the country.

Out of that first month of activity for the Free Huey Defense Fund we managed to muster a press conference. Dr. Price Cobbs, the black psychiatrist who wrote the book, *Black Rage,* made a very brilliant statement, and Dr. Carlton Goodlett, the publisher of the San Francisco black weekly newspaper, *The Sun Reporter,* also spoke on Huey's behalf.

Predictably, some of the same local leaders we couldn't get to do an hour's worth of work, managed to put in an appearance when the television cameras began to grind at the press conference. They were getting a chance to strut like peacocks and wave their fingers at the local white Establishment, thereby more firmly entrenching their positions as dissident blacks and insuring that the local white Establishment would continue to cajole and patronize them. TV nationalism is a form of entertainment that is very popular.

On November 13, 1967, the Alameda County (Oakland) Grand Jury after hearing the evidence presented by the District Attorney's Office, deliberated for twenty-seven minutes and then returned a three-count indictment against Huey. The counts were murder, assault with a deadly weapon on a police officer, and kidnapping. The Grand Jury asked no questions, and no murder weapon was introduced as evidence. They had quickly gotten Huey started on the long road which, they probably felt, would end with the gas chamber.

Representing Huey as legal counsel that afternoon of November 13 was Charles Garry. As a skilled technician—familiar with the processes of criminal jurisprudence—Garry has few peers. His record in cases involving capital punishment is beyond question. He is good—and the men in the penitentiaries whom he kept out of the gas chambers, and those walking the streets, whom he kept out of the penitentiary, will swear to that; and when it really gets down to it, that is the only criterion for a criminal lawyer. However, the selection of Garry, who is white, caused a minor uproar in the camp of the black lawyers in Oakland and San Francisco. The dissenting black lawyers raised the argument that a black lawyer should handle the case of a black man.

I agreed with the argument that these black lawyers were making in theory—but when I considered that a few of these same black lawyers had handled Panther cases prior to Huey, and for the most part conducted the trial work like "Negro Calhouns," I had to disagree in practice. Entrusting Huey's defense to a few of these men would have been tantamount to putting his life in the hands of fools.

Eldridge, myself, and two or three other members of the Huey Newton Defense Fund had a meeting with a group of these black lawyers after the selection of Garry as attorney had been made and the foul odor of bad-mouthing against the Party had begun to circulate throughout the black communities in Oakland and San Francisco.

Most of the black lawyers at that meeting had never done anything for black people, and were aspiring to white values and prestige. In the room that night you did not have one black lawyer with the character and ability of a Howard Moore, the brilliant and dedicated civil rights attorney from Atlanta, Georgia, who has unselfishly contributed many hours in defense of young freedom fighters from SNCC. Instead what you had was a group of opportunists who smelled a chance to get their names out of the society page of black newspapers and into the news sections of the major white newspapers.

We sensed what the whole thing was about, and after the usual amenities were exchanged, there was a light political bantering back and forth between us and the lawyers. They were jockeying for position, and seemed confident that they had the Party on the defensive because of their newly acquired "black bag."

Their confidence was approaching smugness when we finally decided to drop the bombshell on them. We told them that we considered our choice of Charles Garry as Huey's lawyer irreversible, but if they really felt that black lawyers should handle the cases of black men, we had a backlog of legal cases pending on other Party members which we would be very happy to turn over to them individually, or as a committee, if they would form a committee of black lawyers to handle Black Panther cases.

That just about ended the night, and our formal contact with most of these gentlemen. They had been slighted. It was a blow below the belt to suggest they handle common cases, rather than the Newton case which was gaining national publicity by this time (one of the most vocal of this clique, John George, later came under intense fire from the Party for his dubious legal and political dealings that always seemed to be crossing the path of the Panthers).

By the time of his indictment, Huey had been transferred from the hospital ward at San Quentin prison to a cell on the tenth floor of the Alameda County Courthouse in Oakland. Visiting hours were from 1 P.M. to 3 P.M., three times a week. Eldridge kept emphasizing to Party members (who actually needed little prodding) how important it was that we go see Huey at every opportunity, and talk to other black people and tell them to go see Huey, so that our brother's morale would stay high.

The first time I saw Huey, which I believe was the first visiting day, the little hallway leading into the larger visiting room was jammed full of Panthers and friends of Huey. You had to sign a police visiting book, which of course I signed with a phony name.

La Verne Williams, Huey's fiancée, was keeping track of the order in which people came in and limiting the time they spoke. This had to be done because there were so many people there and once they started talking to the brother they wanted to keep rapping—especially the Panthers. Later on, as the trial progressed, La Verne had to make appointments for people to see Huey, because if she didn't, the time would run out before he could talk to all his visitors.

David Hilliard, Bobby Hutton, Emory Douglas, Orlando Harrison, Eldridge, and other Panther brothers were in that line that first day. When I got my chance to talk to Huey, I didn't know what to say at first. I wanted so badly to say the right things to cheer up the brother they had locked in a cage. As I peered through the small barred opening that was supposed to be a window, Huey gave me a clenched fist salute and a smile, and I instantly felt warm all the way through, because the brother was just as I remembered him— always keeping his composure.

It was difficult to talk because you had to talk into a round screened vent-like hole, and then put your ear to a similar device to hear the reply. But we rapped and I got the message, and for the first time since October 28 I felt everything was going to be all right.

After Huey's indictment on November 13, the time was nearing when he was to make an appearance in court for the preliminary stages of his trial. We had to begin to build the machinery which would mobilize people to show up at the courtroom in support of the Minister of Defense whenever he had a trial date.

Erica McClain, a young white radical, who was active in the anarchist politics of the Berkeley, California, community, had known Huey and Bobby Seale from the days when both attended Merritt Junior College in Oakland. She also knew Eldridge, and through him she arranged to set up a committee of sympathetic whites who would support the legal defense of our Minister of Defense.

The committee, which called itself "Honkies for Huey," began to function in the latter part of November. It was largely responsible for writing and printing leaflets announcing Huey's upcoming trial dates. It also printed a flyer called "The Minister of Information Bulletin," which carried a Party political message in connection with information on the trial, and was distributed within the white radical community and the black community, as well as reams of other information on Huey and the Party. In addition it staged many fund raising benefits.

The Party had the manpower but the white radicals had the administrative machinery. Without the machinery provided by the committee, we would not have been able to begin to build and sustain the thousands of supporters of Huey with information and political propaganda. The machinery operated at a high degree of efficiency for the next three months until there was an internal split in the committee—one faction wanted it to become *The White Panthers.*

Eldridge spoke at the first meeting, which was held on a Friday night, at Erica McClain's home in Berkeley.

Speaking softly, as he always did, and emphasizing his points by the use of his hands, Eldridge began to talk about what Huey Newton meant to him. He described the first time he had seen Huey in action, in front of *Ramparts* magazine (this was when the Party was escorting Malcolm X's widow, Betty Shabazz, from the San Francisco airport, to *Ramparts* for an interview with Eldridge). He told how Huey had jacked a shell into his riot shotgun and dared a trigger-happy San Francisco cop to go for his gun.

Eldridge was the person who made Huey come alive and become a revolutionary hero to me. It is very difficult to think of your contemporaries, people who you see, talk to, and share common experiences with everyday as people whose deeds are destined to be recorded by history. I had always had respect for Huey, but now I saw Eldridge elevate him to a level where mere respect would be inappropriate. He made Huey, and what he stood for, something that should be thought of in sacred terms.

Eldridge talked of Huey that night, and he continuously talked of Huey, as the man who picked up the gun and started the revolution—as a contemporary version of the type of black leadership that was best personified by Malcolm X. It was Eldridge who molded the image of Huey Newton. At a later stage, when the Party became a national organization, the image of Huey as a courageous and sincere fighter for black liberation was so well established, that he was looked upon almost as a Messiah by new Panther recruits, while Eldridge was looked upon as the one who had the key to the interpretation of his message, the person instrumental in masterminding the defense of his life. That is why I thought of Eldridge at that time almost as a prophet. Prophets are never sent by themselves, they always come speaking in the name of someone else—Eldridge spoke in the name of Huey.

One Friday, during the first week in December, after we had attended a Friday night meeting of Honkies for Huey, we climbed into Eldridge's Volkswagen bus and started back across the Bay Bridge to San Francisco. There were four of us—Emory Douglas, who is now Minister of Culture for the Party; Kathleen Neal, Eldridge and myself.

I was sitting in the back with Emory, my legs stretched out, trying to sleep. As much as I appreciated what the committee was doing for the Free Huey Movement, I just could not get down with them on the social level. Those Honkies for Huey meetings used to bore me, and I would gulp down wine, hoping to get high enough to thaw out my social contacts with those long-haired white radicals.

I was trying to sleep that night, because it had been one of the nights I had become very high drinking that wine at Erica's place. Eldridge broke into my attempt to sleep.

"Earl, look here brother," he said.

"Yeah," I said, half awake.

"You sleeping nigger," he said, looking back at me through the rear view mirror.

"No, brother, you know I'm not gonna sleep through the revolution," I said. "I'm listening."

Then Eldridge mapped out his strategy for the new Free Huey Defense Fund:

"The Defense Fund is not working. We need to junk the whole thing, and start again. We don't need these other people; the four of us have done more work than all of them put together. I'm going to talk to Melvin Newton, to see about appointing you the Executive Director of the Defense Fund, and we'll just handle it ourselves."

We did talk to Melvin Newton a few days later and he approved the plan. The Huey Newton Defense Fund, of which I was then the Executive Director, was actually an extension of the Party. The reason behind this was that people who could not relate to the Party for whatever reason might possibly relate to the Fund. It was our first step in consciously attempting to build the strongest black organization in California, and then the country.

The night that Eldridge communicated his new plan for the Free Huey Movement was eventful in other ways. As we came off the Bay Bridge, and turned down Laguna Street (I lived there with Abdul Karim, and my cousin Clint Fields) we saw five to ten police cars in a small alley.

Our curiosity was aroused. We circled the block, drove into the alley from the other side, and parked the Volkswagen bus. Eldridge, Emory, and I got out. On one side of the tiny alley were about fifty onlooking black people. Among them were about ten black sisters who were members of the militant Black Student Union at San Francisco State College. In the middle of the alley an ambulance was parked and across the street from where we stood with the other onlookers, ten to fifteen policemen and three ambulance attendants were in a small house. The door was open and we could clearly see what was going on inside.

I asked one of the young brothers there what had happened. He told me that the police had shot a young black brother in this alley and he had managed to crawl into his house. The police claimed that he had robbed an old man on Fell Street, which was just around the corner.

I knew one or two of the young black brothers who lived in that house where the young black brother was lying, his flesh torn by a pig cop's bullet. Six young black brothers lived there, and all were later to become Panthers. The brother who was shot that night became a lieutenant in the San Francisco chapter.

As the ambulance attendants came out of the house, with the young brother on a stretcher, a sister from the BSU group named Jo Anne rushed toward the brother on the stretcher, crying hysterically. She was his girlfriend. One of the cops pushed her back from the stretcher where the brother lay writhing in pain.

When the cop pushed Jo Anne back, Eldridge stepped forward. "Keep your hands off her, you lousy pig motherfucker," he said. It was like a knife cutting through the tension of the two antagonistic camps there, driving them further apart, and making any reconciliation of that dispute extremely difficult.

The white cop Eldridge had shouted at was visibly shaken, and so were his two companions standing near him. One of them went into the house to get support. Eldridge stepped to the middle of the street, a few feet behind the ambulance in which they had put the brother. Emory and I moved up slightly behind him, to his right and left.

"You lousy pig murderers," Eldridge shouted, as the three white cops stood frozen in their tracks a few feet from us. We were not packing guns; in fact we probably didn't have a fingernail file among us. I wondered what they would do if they knew we were unarmed.

I could sense that the crowd of black people was moving closer together behind us. It is in this type of situation, when black people catch the police in their community with the blood of a black person they have shot still dripping on their hands, and some mad black man or black woman begins a heated exchange with these vile intruders, that revolts in the black ghettoes are touched off.

"You are going to die—
"We are going to kill you—
"We are going to kill your racist ass."

The black sisters from the San Francisco State Black Student Union had started a rhythmic chant, using the style which had been made famous by LeRoi Jones.

Within a few seconds after one of the white cops had gone into the house to get support, this big black cop came out. He was about 6 feet 5 inches, and must have weighed 250 pounds.

He advanced toward Eldridge with five or six white cops who had regained their courage behind him. Eldridge accepted the challenge, and quickly called his hand.

"You Uncle Tom, black ass pig motherfucker," he shouted, pointing at the black cop. The black cop stopped in his tracks a safe distance from Eldridge.

It was a showdown. The pigs were about seven, and they were edgy enough to become trigger-happy. There were three of us (Eldridge, Emory, and myself), although I'm sure that if anything went down we would have had the rest of the black people there with us. When I look back on that night, I'm sure that is what stopped them from putting bullets in the brains of all three of us.

"You're an Uncle Tom! A lackey for the man! A bootlicker!" Eldridge spat these epithets at the black cop the cowardly white cops had sicked on him.

"You're the Uncle Tom!" the black cop shot back. When he said that, I knew that the showdown was a Mexican standoff. When you have the firepower, as the police did that night, and you have to result to wolfing with your antagonist, then you have gone for the bluff.

The situation calmed down in a few minutes. The black cop's companions pulled him away. We left the scene, and Jo Anne was allowed to ride in the ambulance to the hospital with her boyfriend.

That night we won many new recruits to the Party. When they saw Eldridge shout down the police and intimidate them, they became instant converts. The policeman is almost omnipotent in the black community, and when a black man challenges that power and his name does not end up on a tombstone somewhere, he becomes a popular leader to a large number of people.

Huey's second appearance in court was in early December. A couple of days before that court appearance, a few of us were at Weldon Stroud's apartment working on some propaganda on the trial appearance, when we received a telephone call from a lawyer who was connected with Bobby Seale's case. He informed us that Bobby was in the process of being released from Santa Rita prison.

At first I was wary. Bobby was supposed to serve six months, and they were letting him out after five. Any leniency by police and prison authorities puts me on my guard; but particularly in this case. The support for Huey was building astronomically in the Bay Area, and then they let Bobby on the loose to act as a catalyst to push this movement to even greater dimensions.

I thought it was too good to be true, and that they were trying to set us up for a conspiracy bust (that winter they had made two mass conspiracy arrests against the Revolutionary Action Movement). I figured that they would let Bobby out and then arrest the remaining Party leadership *en masse*—then go lying to the public that we were planning to break Huey out of jail. It would be perfect, for people knew how close Huey and Bobby were, and it would not be too difficult to build a case that Bobby had led a plot to rescue his closest comrade. They never did pull the conspiracy game on us at that stage, although I'm sure their strategy in letting Bobby loose was to set it up.

Fortunately, at that time the leadership of the Party was a small, tight-knit group. That closed the main avenue down which the law enforcement agencies could work—the avenue by which they send in their spies suggesting fantastic revolutionary deeds and seducing an organization into making preparations for them. I've talked to many brothers who have been trapped in the conspiracy game, and they always swear that that is the way it goes down.

Huey's second trial appearance was on a Friday, and at nine o'clock in the morning. I was there at about 8 A.M. and already there were a couple of hundred young black and white people milling around outside the Alameda County Courthouse. In the flyers that we distributed informing people about the trial appearance, we asked that they come out early so that we could be sure that the courtroom would be packed with Huey's supporters.

The majority of the people who had turned out early were students or young activists. Many young black revolutionary brothers and sisters from San Francisco State were there; as were their white radical counterparts from the Berkeley campus of the University of California. These students were to sustain their support for Huey and increase their numbers throughout the entire trial, which was to run for almost a year. Also there were black activists from the Bay Area, who realized once it was upon them, that how we waged the struggle for Huey's life was going to be a major factor in the development of the political revolutionary fervor in the Bay Area.

As planned, the courtroom was filled to capacity, and all were Huey supporters; except possibly some of the Establishment newspaper people, the bailiffs, and court reporters. The stoic and staid countenances of well-groomed Establishment types, who usually predominate at sensational trials, were replaced by those of enthusiastic and vital long-haired white radicals, and Afro-coiffeured black revolutionaries. It was to be a pro-Huey audience each trial date throughout the ten month trial. There was a tenseness and excitement in the courtroom that morning as the people waited to glimpse Huey. It was an audience made up of people who were never to wane in their open display of enthusiasm for Huey.

At the end of the trial when the jury was getting ready to hand down the decision on Huey's life, the pro-Huey supporters had already made their decision, which absolved Huey of any crime, and had written thousands of words about their decision in radical underground newspapers, while also spreading the message by word of mouth; and these black revolutionaries and white radicals could not be accused of being uninformed, for they had been present at each trial date. The argument that pro-Huey backers were politically partial was easily dismissed with the counterargument that the Establishment news media, to whom the American people are slaves, are also politically partial.

As Huey entered the courtroom he raised his right arm and gave a clenched fist salute which was returned by most of the people present. Then Huey and Charles Garry faced the judge's bench, and the first session of his trial began.

It lasted less than thirty minutes. While Garry was going through the legal maneuvers with the prosecutor, the Alameda County (Oakland) Assistant District Attorney, and the Judge, Huey would be turning sideways to glance at the courtroom audience. Whenever he recognized a Panther brother in the courtroom audience, he would give a clenched fist salute and the Panther would return it. This must have been done a dozen times that day. When he saw his fiancée La Verne Williams in the audience, he acknowledged her by putting his hand to his mouth and throwing her a kiss.

After the trial session was completed, and Huey was escorted out, the people in the courtroom emptied into the corridor just outside the courtroom. The corridor was packed with other Huey supporters who had not been able to get into the courtroom because it was filled to capacity. At each trial session during the duration of the ten-month trial, scores of people would pack this corridor wearing their Free Huey buttons, and causing a major security worry for the guards who had to keep the crowd orderly.

When I went downstairs, I saw Bobby Seale on the first floor. People were greeting him, one after the other, genuinely happy that he was back on the scene again. It was the first time I had seen Bobby in five months, and I walked up and we shook each other's hands, and exchanged some warm brotherly greetings. It was good to see Bobby back and I knew it would be a stimulus to the Party members, because Bobby was the co-founder and probably the best organizer that the Party had, particularly since they had Huey in the slammers.

I walked outside and stood in front of the courthouse for a few minutes, watching the demonstration for Huey which was in full progress. There were a couple of hundred people that day (at the peak of Huey's trial, there would be upward of five thousand people at the courthouse). The people were walking in a circle in front of the courthouse, holding cardboard placards with *Free Huey* on them, and singing in unison: *Free Huey, and Jail the Pigs.*

The demonstration outside the courthouse had been going on since before the trial session started, and about fifteen minutes after the trial session had ended, the people were called together in front of the courthouse by Eldridge and Bobby, who stood on the courthouse steps and addressed them.

You could feel the inspiration that the people received when Bobby Seale talked to them. It was good to see an organization and its leaders pledge their uncompromising support to one of their own.

"We're going to get down to the nitty-gritty," Bobby said that day, "and we ain't gonna miss no nits, and no grits."

| 5 |

One day in December right after Huey's second trial appearance, Eldridge and I were riding around San Francisco in his Volkswagen bus, doing some routine Panther business, when we spotted a sound truck announcing an upcoming voter registration rally to be given in San Francisco by the Peace and Freedom Party. It was the first time I had heard of this organization.

By now our administrative machinery was functioning very smoothly, and we were able to print and distribute thousands of leaflets each week, as well as make and answer hundreds of phone calls requesting information on the trial. Also we had produced and sold thousands of buttons, with the message: *Free Huey; Huey Must Be Set Free*. But when we saw that Peace and Freedom sound truck the same thought must have flashed simultaneously through Eldridge's mind and mine, for we looked at each other and smiled. Eldridge pulled the Volkswagen bus over to the curb, and we paused a minute and watched it move slowly up Fillmore Avenue, which is in the heart of San Francisco's black ghetto, telling anybody within earshot, loud and clear and unmistakably, the time, place, and purpose of the rally.

"It really would be nice if we had that sound truck to announce Huey's trial dates," Eldridge said, expressing the thought which had lodged in both our minds.

"We could righteously take care of business," I said.

The only thing that remained to be decided was exactly how we were going to get the use of that truck. We discussed the possibility of physically intimidating the Peace and Freedom Party into letting us use it, but that idea was quickly discarded as being politically unsophisticated. So the only alternative was to make contact with key people in the Peace and Freedom Party, and see if we could negotiate an arrangement to share the truck with them. (The following August, when Eldridge talked about this simple beginning of the coalition to a University of Southern California audience, they were amazed, for they probably felt that the coalition was entered into after working out elaborate theoretical considerations and pondering upon all the possible consequences.)

A meeting with the Peace and Freedom people was arranged a few days later at Eldridge's apartment (it was very easy to bring this about, since the Party had inroads into the white radical social and political network). I was at the apartment along with Eldridge and Emory Douglas. Eldridge wanted me to conduct the preliminary negotiations, setting the tone for more extensive talks in the future. The fact that he worked for *Ramparts* magazine, which was part of the Establishment Left, would have made it difficult for him to drive a hard bargain. He had either worked for or socialized with most of the organizers of the Peace and Freedom Party. Eldridge, however, definitely had the knack of handling white radicals. To a large degree, his ascendancy as a key figure in the black liberation movement was due to the support for him on the white Establishment Left. I always felt that he put too much faith in white radicals and gave them more than their due.

As I became more familiar with the white radical movement, I noticed that there is a certain group of individuals whom one might call the Establishment Left, who drift from one cause to another, organize one leftist organization after another, gaining prestige and influence in certain circles, and sometimes fame and fortune in the larger scope of American life.

That afternoon two of these people, who were organizers of the Peace and Freedom Party, came to Eldridge's apartment. Sator, the younger one (I never knew what his first name was), had been in the joint with Eldridge, was in his mid-twenties, and had the look and mannerisms of a "hip" white boy—the type who comes from almost the same set of conditions as blacks, and adopts a life style which is most commonly seen in the black ghettoes. He struck me as a type of political hustler, although I really liked him as a person. The other organizer, Morton Vickers, was probably in his late forties or early fifties. He later told me he had been an organizer for leftist causes since the labor movement. (He acted as a personal guide and aide for Kathleen Cleaver and me later that summer when were were in Honolulu.) When Vickers told me how long he had been in various left movements, I couldn't help but feel sorry for him, for it seemed that others who had started with him had moved on to bigger and better things, and he was still on the rank and file level.

Sator and Vickers explained to me that the Peace and Freedom Party was trying to have its name placed on the California ballot for the Presidential election year of 1968. They had to have so many thousands of California residents who were eligible to vote register as members. All of this had to be accomplished by the middle of January, which was less than a month away, and they were running behind schedule.

Like all other factions within the Establishment Left, this fledgling party was depending upon the black community to put its thing over. Sator and Vickers explained that the Peace and Freedom Party wanted to kick off an intensified voter registration drive in the black community in San Francisco and Oakland within a week's time.

Their plan of operation was to go into the black areas like Hunters Point and Potrero Hill with their sound trucks, announcing a rally, where they thought "it would be good if a Black Panther would talk," as well as one of their people. There would be a table at the rally where the people could register for the Peace and Freedom Party. They also thought it would be good to have a couple of Black Panthers there as registrars.

After they had carefully explained what interests of theirs they wanted served, I countered by beginning to explain how we felt they should reciprocate. I told Sator and Vickers that our main concern at that point was being able to gather enough resources to successfully mount the defense for Huey's life. We were short on everything: money, printing equipment, sound trucks, etc. I wanted it to be clear to them that any help we gave them in getting registrars from the black community had to be solely based upon whether or not they could give us the resources we needed, and not upon any idealistic notions on our part about supporting on principle alone any attempt to pump new blood into the archaic and ineffective American two-party political system.

The northern California organizing committee of the Peace and Freedom Party, which was the decision-making organ for that area, was meeting that evening, and it was decided that the talks should be resumed then.

The meeting that night was held in a big, rundown building, on a sidestreet that runs parallel to Market Street—the main street in the downtown section of San Francisco. This same building was used for meetings of the radical white-dominated anti-war movement. It seemed to be the physical and political hub of white radical activity in the Bay Area.

The eight or so members of the organizing committee were going through an agenda of their routine business when Eldridge and I arrived. Quickly they wound up what they were doing, so that they could get down to the more important business we had come there to discuss with them—the possibility of the Panthers and the Peace and Freedom Party working together. The discussion began very cautiously, for there was a fragile area of understanding between us that could have been permanently shattered by either side being stubbornly aggressive.

That summer of 1967 most of the hard core white radicals had gone to Chicago to the New Politics Convention, with well laid plans and dubious intentions to reconcile with their black brothers on the left the splits which had developed between them after the cry for Black Power the previous summer, when whites had been unceremoniously kicked out of the black liberation movement and told to go do their own thing in the white community. The white radicals had devised this New Politics Convention, hoping to bring everybody back together under the banner of the broad philosophy of American needing a type of new politics, knowing well that people would be becoming more politically conscious with the presidential election coming up in '68. They counted on this immediate concern being a cohesive force in mending the splits between blacks and whites on the left.

This manuever on the part of the politically power conscious white radicals, and particularly their leadership on the Establishment Left, was a rearguard action intended not only to bring them back into the black liberation movement, but to place them at the head of it. If a coalition could have been worked out in Chicago, the white left would have had the balance of voting power since there were more white delegates there; and they would also have determined the political priority in the movement, since the ominous 1968 presidential election was right around the corner.

But they miscalculated the political maturity and aggressiveness of the black people they were dealing with. The black revolutionaries pulled a *black caucus* on the whites, saying that they would determine what they considered the political priorities for black people. And they decided that they would choose their own representatives from within the caucus, not the floor of the body politic, and that the representation from the blacks would be equal with the whites.

The whites were now completely outfoxed. They had to

beg the blacks to come back, so that they would save face with the white conservative Establishment. The conservatives knew that their brothers on the Left had no power, but if they were to lose face because of a black political uprising, the mystique of the white Left having influence in the black-oriented movement, and therefore a sphere of influence in American politics, would have been crushed.

The New Politics Convention blew the game of the white Left Establishment. They came back from Chicago licking their wounds, with their heads bowed, asking "what went wrong?" I believe that each one of them must have taken a solemn vow to himself never again to be put into a position where a black man individually, or black men collectively, would cause such embarassment.

It was this type of attitude, the direct result of the New Politics fiasco and other ego-deflating political defeats at the hands of blacks within the short span of time since '66, that created the atmosphere of suspicion and caution that hung in the air in that dingy hall the first night that Eldridge and I met with the northern California organizing committee of the Peace and Freedom Party.

We explained to them that the only way the two organizations would be able to work together in a coalition, would be if the party defined the program that would be presented in the black community. That we could not be privy to any coalition which allowed white people to cross the boundaries into the black community to define to black people what should be their political program.

Our plan of action caught them off guard. The Peace and Freedom people had obviously hoped to make a coalition where we would agree on certain broad principles and then serve as their entrée into the black community, where they would be able to run their program.

One of their organizers, a bespectacled white youth, openly expressed what must have been the secret thoughts of the others, judging by the looks of relief on their faces when he spoke. He objected to our plan, saying that the Panther

Party would be defining Peace and Freedom's program, if we were permitted to control what was said in the black community.

Eldridge then made a skillful argument. It was the basis for a position paper that he was to write later, called "Revolution in the White Mother Country, National Liberation in the Colony," which was a definitive statement of the interrelationships of blacks and whites in changing the economic, social, and political fabric of America. He told the whites there that if any coalition was to be formed, it had to be conceived with the understanding that each organization would do its own thing because there are different sets of problems in the black and white communities, and the people from these respective communities know best the most effective solutions to their own problems. Therefore the black organization would work with the problems and solutions in the black community, and the white organization would work with the problems and solutions in the white community. The necessity for a coalition would develop out of specific purposes that one group could more easily attain by cooperating with the other. In the case of this proposed coalition, the Party wanted to build massive support for Huey's defense, and Peace and Freedom wanted to gain electoral political support in the black community. But the roles that blacks and whites would play in such a coalition could not be interchangeable; blacks would speak to black issues, and whites would have to limit themselves to white issues.

Eldridge's argument stymied them. They had to go for it in principle, so they reluctantly agreed. Actually they had no other choice, because if they had a coalition agreement with the Panthers, people could not tag them as being just an offshoot of the two major political parties. They badly wanted the image of being radical, and they knew that by working with the Panthers they would get it.

I asked them if it would be too premature to talk about Huey, since his cause was our political priority, and we wanted both parties at the meeting to immediately begin to put their combined efforts into the Free Huey Movement. The bespectacled white youth again objected. He argued that the people there were only an organizing committee and could not make a decision to support Huey. All that could be done was for them to make a recommendation at the meeting of the entire Peace and Freedom Party in March. This white youth was the only one of the organizers playing power politics. His doubts clearly showed that his primary concern was keeping the important decision making in the hands of the PFP. He must have sensed that they were moving into a trap.

Again Eldridge came to the forefront. He talked of the limited amount of time that we had to build the Free Huey Movement; flipping the coin on the other side, he reminded the Peace and Freedom people that they had less than a month to qualify for the California ballot, and they needed support in the black communities. He warned them that procrastination would work more to their disadvantage than ours, and our support was only forthcoming on the grounds that they begin to support Huey immediately.

The white youth did not waver; in fact he became obstinate. He said that in effect the Panther Party would be deciding a platform for Peace and Freedom, which they would be committed to before the entire body met. It was clear that he was looking for a political deadlock, which would give him valuable time to de-escalate the support among his fellow colleagues that we enjoyed at the present. But such a deadlock was not coming.

Eldridge let loose with the knockout punch that went right to his political solar plexis—his revolutionary consciousness. "Actually we are arguing over power that neither one of us has," Eldridge said. "But if Peace and Freedom calls itself revolutionary, or even radical, and not a product of traditional American politics, it should realize that the revolutionary fervor comes from the most oppressed class— which is black people. And any political party, which is supposedly revolutionary or radical, and not just on vacation from the Democratic Party, would support the vanguard of the oppressed, which is what the Panthers are."

That shut up our dissenter. If there is anything white radicals hate to be accused of, it is of not being serious about changing the American system. And that is because they are shaky—America leaves so many openings for whites to fluidly move back into respectability. We had won. The Peace and Freedom people really did not have a program anyway. Therefore by accepting our concrete program they at least had something to do.

They agreed that they would push the Free Huey Movement. So we got down to the tactics of how they should do it. It was decided that they would print a leaflet about Huey's case with the political message, *Can A Black Man Have A Fair Trial?,* and both parties could distribute it. Also, we would man the sound trucks announcing a voters' registration rally in Hunters Point (our people, of course, would use the opportunity to talk about Huey).

On December 22, 1967, the joint rally sponsored by the Black Panther Party and Peace and Freedom Party was held in Hunters Point. It was actually the unveiling of the controversial coalition, and it marked the end of our honeymoon in the black community in general, and the black liberation movement in particular. Since '66, the *modus operandi* of the movement had been to exclude whites. The coalition came in for sharp criticism, publicly and privately, from many quarters.

At the rally that day, Bobby Seale spoke for the Panther Party. Bob Avakian, a white radical who is the son of an Oakland judge, and who later became Eldridge's campaign manager in his candidacy for the presidency of America on the Peace and Freedom ticket, spoke for Peace and Freedom. Some psychedelic rock band also played.

Not only had we gotten the use of the sound trucks, but we now had the full support of the northern California

Peace and Freedom Party, which was by far the strongest white radical group in California, and soon to have national apparatus. The support of the northern California group forced the hand of the less organized Peace and Freedom chapters across California, and later the nation. The Peace and Freedom Party was to replace Honkies for Huey as our administrative machinery, and we were to set its political direction.

I was home in Los Angeles during the Christmas holidays of 1967. It was then that I first met Alprentice Carter. He was called Bunchy; like a "bunch of greens." We were later to work very closely together on the central staff of the Los Angeles Panther chapter.

One night Eldridge, Kathleen, and I went over to the Teen Post on 87th Street and Central Avenue, in Los Angeles, where Bunchy worked as head counselor. The Teen Post was an anti-poverty youth program; and many of our first recruits in the Los Angeles Panther chapter were from it (including a young brother named Tommy Lewis, or "Little Tommy," who was later to die a violent death, murdered in a gas station that summer by the Los Angeles police).

We entered the Teen Post by climbing a flight of rickety stairs at the back of the building to the second floor. After we knocked on the door it was a few minutes before a voice demanded, "Who is it?" We identified ourselves and Bunchy's assistant, a crazy nigger named Terry, opened the door and let us in, still holding the .38 caliber snub nosed pistol with its hammer cocked (I still don't know who Terry was expecting). We spent the night talking—Eldridge, Kathleen, Bunchy, Terry, and I. Most of the talk centered around how best to move a Panther chapter into Los Angeles. Bunchy and Terry explained that they had territorial control over a certain piece of "turf."

We also drank wine. A drink that Bunchy and Terry called "the bitter dog" or "the bitter motherfucker." It was red port wine, mixed with a can of concentrated lemon juice.

This was later to become a popular drink among the Panthers. In fact I used to say that the initial two things that the Los Angeles chapter gave to the Party were the drink "the bitter motherfucker" and the expression "right on."

Bunchy had been in the joint with Eldridge, and as he told me later he really got "turned on" by Eldridge when he read the essay "The Primeval Mitosis" (later included in *Soul On Ice*). Bunchy idolized Eldridge, and I could understand that, Eldridge being the prime example of how an ex-convict could move to the center stage of life. (You often find ex-convicts having a strong indentification with Malcolm X for the same reason.) Eldridge had told me about his "partner," Bunchy before I met him. I found him as "crazy" as Eldridge had said. (When I use the term, "crazy," I do so in the sense that it is used on the streets by the brothers, and it is a flattering term.) Bunchy was "a classic street nigger." In other words, he was a very polished model of a certain life style. As a teenager he had been the leader of one of the most notorious youth gangs in Los Angeles, the Slausons. He had a long Afro hairstyle, and in his classic street manner, he would hold a bottle of wine in one hand, hitch up his pants with the other, cock his head, and go into long dissertation, on practically any subject—dissertations which many times seemed to border on madness, but his madness was the spiritual truth of the lives of black people. Bunchy didn't go to prison for anything small, he was going all the way. He went to prison for bank robbery. Bunchy had style.

On Christmas day of 1967, Eldridge and Kathleen came over to my parents' home. We ate and talked there. Then we went over to Eldridge's parents' house in Altadena, which is a suburb of Pasadena. We ate more turkey, and talked more.

I believe it was two days after Christmas that I got a call from Eldridge. He asked if I could come over that morning, there were some important things happening. I told him I wouldn't be able to make it until the afternoon, for I had made some important commitments.

I was later than expected, and I didn't see Eldridge and

Kathleen until that evening. Meanwhile, a few things had changed. Eldridge and Kathleen had been married that afternoon, in a private ceremony somewhere on Los Angeles' eastside. Bunchy and his brother Glen were the witnesses.

As the year 1968 came in we began thinking about having a rally in Oakland to raise money for the Huey Newton Defense Fund, and to focus national attention on the defense work we were doing on the west coast. Although the incident with Huey and the police had received national coverage when it happened and there had been some national coverage of the first few trial dates; the phenomenon of the Huey Newton defense was still mostly a west coast matter. There had been tacit concern for Huey within the black liberation movement, but a functional involvement was lacking. Probably it was due to the fact that other leaders of the black liberation movement, H. Rap Brown, Max Stanford, Herman Ferguson, LeRoi Jones, Cleveland Sellers, were also entrenched in defense work, and the efforts within the movement had to be spread among them.

In discussing the plans for the rally, Eldridge brought forth the idea of having Stokely Carmichael as the keynote speaker. It was a logical choice. Stokely had just capped off his tenure as chairman of SNCC by globe-trotting around the world in the summer and fall of 1967 hanging America's dirty linen out to air at a time when she could least afford it —the cities of America were being laid seiged that summer by black people, and the Vietnamese war was escalating.

Stokely had just returned to the U.S. in December, and he had said he was not going to speak publicly inside the country. But there was a great demand to hear him, and Eldridge felt confident he could convince him to speak at a rally for Huey.

We had two things in our favor. Stokely had been drafted into the Black Panther Party in July 1967 as an honorary field marshal; during the same time that he was chairman of SNCC and publicly making a stand against being drafted into the U.S. Army. When we called Stokely and told him that he had been drafted by the Party into our army of black liberation he had said: "You can't draft me, I enlist." The second thing in our favor, was that Eldridge had traveled with Stokely for more than a month to do a story on him for *Ramparts* magazine, and Stokely usually listened to his counsel.

We set a tentative date in January for the rally. Then we began what was to turn into a series of calls to the New York SNCC office to establish contact with Carmichael. There were some internal hassles going on between Carmichael and the SNCC central committee (they were later to fire Stokely from the organization), and it was impossible to establish his whereabouts.

In the course of this series of calls, SNCC's New York office, and particularly James Forman, began to suggest to us the possibility of expanding the rally to include other people. We were very much for it, and we began to tinker with the idea of a rally which would have a much broader importance than the one originally planned. Carmichael was finally contacted in Boston, and he agreed to speak at the rally. (A couple of weeks later, Eldridge and Bobby went to Washington D.C. to tie up the details with him.)

Eldridge was the one who recognized the possibilities of what we might be getting into. He said we should not have the rally in January but should schedule it for February 17, which was a Saturday. And it should be held at the Oakland Auditorium, only a stone's throw from the Oakland County Jail, where Huey was incarcerated.

February 17—at first the significance of that date did not dawn upon me. February 17 was Huey's birthday. The affair was being transformed from a rally to what was to become a birthday celebration for Huey, with most of the nationally prominent leaders in the black liberation movement attending to express their support for the Minister of Defense of the Black Panther Party, Huey P. Newton.

| 6 |

I went back to Los Angeles in early January 1968. I was under orders from the Central Committee to organize a *Free Huey Birthday Celebration* in Los Angeles on February 18. At that time our only chapter was in the San Francisco-Oakland area, and I was instructed to get with Bunchy and see about getting the Party officially started in L.A.

It had been four and a half years since I had finished undergraduate school at the University of Southern California and gone to San Francisco to go to law school. I had come back to L.A. to stay this time, to a different life than the one I had left. It is not far in terms of physical distance from the University of Southern California's campus to Central and Broadway Avenues, "main stems" of L.A.'s black ghetto. But for a black man the trip is a very long one when you think of it in terms of customs and values.

My base of operations in L.A. was to be the neighborhoods surrounding Broadway and Central Avenues—the area you might call "nigger-town." Later, when I was an official on the central staff of the L.A. chapter, I noticed a deep-seated suspicion on the part of the black brothers and sisters from the neighborhoods around Central and Broadway Avenues, which is called the eastside, toward black brothers and sisters who came from the westside of L.A. The blacks who went to schools such as USC and UCLA, usually came from the westside. This suspicion was the effect of the economic class structure. The westside was representative of the black bourgeoisie; the eastside, of the masses, and there was very little interaction, social or political, between these two elements of black society.

Having originally come from the westside of L.A., I knew that most of the college-trained blacks were not willing to sacrifice for the movement what they had struggled all their lives to gain. The members of this class were afflicted with their own kind of suffering—a psychological deterioration resulting from the realization that their existence had no end in itself and was only justified by approval from the interloper, the white world—which was ironically now snubbing those who had "Uncle Tommed" so hard, to listen to the uneducated blacks from the eastside.

On the other side of the coin, I was to see a strong tendency within the black masses on the eastside who were in the gutters and sewers of life, to be *aspiring bourgeoisie*. Although they criticized the bourgeoisie, many of these young black brothers and sisters were striving to get the same things they condemned. Their criticism therefore had a tinge of jealousy.

I felt that the natural place to being to organize the Free Huey Birthday Celebration was L.A.'s Black Congress, a loosely structured body of black organizations comprising a full range of political persuasions from the conservative NAACP, to Ron Karenga's black nationalist US.

The Black Congress had stated its purpose as "operational black unity" but I was soon to find out its real function—*it was a meeting place to establish protocol for the power groups in the organized black community* (or in what order —determined by relative power—organizations should be recognized as spokesmen for the black liberation movement in Los Angeles). With so many differences within the movement, plus pressures from without, the Congress had come to serve as a safety valve against the possibility of an organization taking rash action to prove a point. (That point usually being that "I am King of the Mountain," the leader of the black people in L.A.) The Congress allowed organizations the opportunity to prove a point, if possible, in a civilized and brotherly way rather than resorting to internal gang fighting or petty name calling.

Although the Party had made several informal scouting ventures into the L.A. area, the official announcement of an L.A. base of operations was tentatively set to coincide with Huey's birthday celebration. We were going to kick off the chapter in grand style.

A few days after I had setttled in L.A., I spoke to a business session of the Black Congress. Bunchy and Terry (his partner from the Teen Post) went with me to that meeting. It was going to be necessary to convince the Black Congress to support the Free Huey Celebration, and if possible set up a Huey Newton Defense Fund. We weren't strong enough to accomplish this by ourselves since we had neither the organization in the black community, nor an organized support group in the white radical community.

It is always difficult to come into a new territory, and if that territory is a big, organized city like Los Angeles, you need good contacts and have to be able to establish a good rapport with the strong organizations already on the "turf." You can't have these powers band together, to isolate you before you get in motion.

At the Black Congress that night I explained to the member organizations that we were planning a birthday celebration for Huey Newton on Saturday, February 17, in Oakland, and that Stokely Carmichael would be the guest of honor, making his first public appearance since his widely discussed international tour.

I told them that the Party would also like to celebrate brother Huey's birthday with the black people of the Los Angeles area the following day, February 18, and thus make a show of statewide solidarity and brotherhood.

Everything went very smoothly. There was a consensus to support the celebration. Huey was a living martyr to most of the people involved in the movement on the west coast, and those early days were a honeymoon period between the Panthers and other organizations in the black liberation movement.

The motion to sponsor the Free Huey Birthday Celebration was put on the floor by Ron Karenga, or "the Maluana" as he is called by his organization, and in those days the direction in which the Maluana Ron Karenga swayed was the direction in which the Black Congress swayed. This was understandable, for Karenga's US was the best organized and disciplined group in L.A., and the only organization with a uniform ideology, and most important, with an army. (This army was called The Young Simbas—Simbas is Swahili for *lions*.) At that time the Los Angeles "turf" was almost the exclusive domain of US, since there was no organization or individual within or without the Black Congress which was strong enough to be its equal politically or militarily. But the Panthers soon began to gain strength and challenge its power, and the first signs of bad blood developed. This rivalry was to develop into a power struggle of tragic proportions. (As Kwame Nkrumah once wrote: *"When two elephants fight, only the grass gets hurt."*)

That first night at the Black Congress helped us to establish our rapport with the powers in the L.A. area. The Party was fortunate too in having Bunchy already there, and he was very successful in organizing the young black brothers on the street. In fact, he had built us an army of these young black brothers within a few months.

About a week or so after this meeting, the Party was able to officially announce that it had set up an L.A. chapter. The occasion was a Sunday afternoon poetry reading of black poets, which was being held at the Black Congress.

I was at the reading with Bunchy, his brother Arthur (usually known as Glen), and about twenty young brothers who were the first L.A. recruits—the number was soon to swell to a couple of hundred. Bunchy had been appointed Deputy Minister of Defense for southern California. He was the first deputy in the Party to be appointed by the Central Committee in Oakland and approved by Huey. With the appointment of Bunchy in L.A., the Party was beginning to develop a regional staff according to a pattern we were to follow in city after city across the country, as we expanded into a national organization. On this staff the Deputy Minister of Defense was usually the top ranking official in any given area, since the Party had from the beginning defined itself as being in a "state of war."

At the poetry reading that Sunday afternoon, Bunchy read some of his poetry. He closed his reading with his poem, *Black Mother,* the final lines of which read:

> "for a slave of natural death who dies
> can't balance out to two dead flies
> I'd rather be without the shame
> A bullet lodged within my brain
> if I were not to reach our goal
> let bleeding cancer torment my soul."

After reading his poetry, Bunchy hitched up his pants, threw back his head and announced that the Black Panther Party had come to L.A. He also assured the audience of about forty black culture buffs that they didn't have to worry about the police kicking in the door of the Black Congress that afternoon. If they did so, it would be the last door that they kicked in.

The following day, Walter Bremond, the Chairman of the Black Congress, called and asked me and Bunchy to attend a meeting that afternoon at Bob's Drive-in Restaurant on Figueroa Drive. Ron Karenga's US organization was represented there by two members of its hierarchy. John Floyd, who was a member of a very small group which called itself the Black Panther Political Party was also at the meeting. Bremond was the mediator.

At the meeting, US accused a Party member of making slanderous remarks against Ron Karenga. There was also the accusation that Party members were referring to Karenga's people as "those niggers with the bongos in their ears."* US was attempting to extract an apology for the statements.

Although there was no apology, for there had been no official Party dictum derogatorily referring to Maluana Ron Karenga, the meeting was not unpleasant. (I must say that most of Karenga's people with whom I have had contact are easily approachable; many are brothers and sisters right off the block.) There was no hostility apparent when we left the drive-in that afternoon.

One night a few days after that meeting, a shooting scrap developed between a small group of Party members and a small group of US members. Nobody was killed, but two Panthers and one member of US suffered minor wounds.

After this, the hostile feeling between the Party and US flared to such a level, that it was difficult to keep our forces in check. Our nucleus of young brothers felt that Karenga's people had provoked the shooting affair, and they waited the order from the L.A. leadership to retaliate.

It was a touch-and-go situation. Many of the young brothers in Karenga's organization were from eastside youth gangs. The young Panther cadre were from the same, or rival, gangs.

There had been contact and rivalry between these young brothers before, and the rumored recent hostilities between the leaders of the two organizations had floated down to their level. Since they came from the same neighborhoods, there was immediate friction when they happened to run across each other and both sides felt obligated to defend their respective camps, regardless of whether there were orders to do so. By the code of the street, this was known as gang fighting,

---

* Bongos are an African type drum, and the reference was to a slang phrase to signify a cultural nationalist.

and they had been gang fighters long before they were nationalists.

The situation deteriorated so quickly, that work toward
the Free Huey Birthday Celebration came to a standstill.
There was an atmosphere of impending doom, as L.A.
seemed to be drawing close to a fratricidal war between the
Panthers and US, with other member organizations having
to pick their sides.

It was at the height of this tension that James Forman, the
black liberation leader from SNCC, came to town to be a
keynote speaker at a rally put on by the New Politics Convention.

After arriving in L.A., he heard the news buzzing through
the black ghettoes of the impending holocaust, and the Black
Panther Political Party asked him to intercede (from what I
found out later, they felt they were being squeezed in the
struggle between US and the Party; a few weeks later, the
Black Panther Political Party yielded to certain pressure and
advice, dropped that name, and became the friends of
SNCC).

I had met Forman in New York that summer. He renewed
acquaintance with me, and talked to me about the difficulties. Then he proceeded to talk to Karenga to hear the other
side of the dispute.

Armed with views from both sides, Forman went up to San
Francisco to talk to the Central Committee of the Black Panther Party. He succeeded in convincing Bobby and Eldridge
to come to L.A., and try and bring a halt to the confusion,
and get the preparations for the Free Huey Birthday Celebration moving again.

Bobby and Eldridge and an entourage of Panther brothers went to L.A., and a general session was held at the Black
Congress. Eldridge talked about "being able to put our
difficulties aside, and giving the next few weeks to Huey . . .
anybody who could not relate to Huey, we should give a one-
way ticket to the State of Idaho." I could see then that things

were about to return to normal, for the sight of the Panther Central Committee making a special trip to L.A. to assure the member organizations of the Black Congress that they were interested in "peace" and making the Free Huey Birthday Celebration a success, brought confidence to everyone. It also swung support back to the Party, and if that had not happened, I feel that the Free Huey Celebration in L.A. would not have come off.

Forman talked inspiringly that night. He said that we should start putting a price on our leaders, to make it expensive for the Establishment to meddle with them. He gave examples to illustrate his point, including himself. The price he had set for his own life, "was one hundred lives of the enemy, plus ten police stations wiped off the map." It is out of that Forman dictum that we later framed our now famous battle cry: *If Huey Goes the Sky's The Limit.*

Things were back on an even keel. A committee drawn from the member organizations of the Black Congress was formed to handle the organizing of the birthday celebration. I was pulled off the assignment, and the L.A. Panther chapter was instructed just to oversee the planning.

Bobby, Eldridge, and the Panthers who had come down with them from National Headquarters, stayed in town for about five days. Forman also stayed to assist in any way that he could.

The organization of the L.A. chapter was to be the first Panther endeavor to expand outside the Bay area. Because L.A. was the largest city in California, with the greatest black population, it was important not to blunder again, after our awkward first attempts. If L.A. was sewn up, then the Party could claim dominance in the largest state, California, and begin to spread across America. Acquiring a foothold there was an integral part of what you might call *Panther Domino Theory.* *

---

* During the summer of '68, when the L.A. chapter was at its peak, it was to number over four hundred people, and was second

In those five days we accomplished a lot. Every day was occupied with meetings with the Free Huey Celebration Committee, and key discussions between the L.A. leadership cadre, National Headquarters Central Committee, and Forman around the issue of internal structuring of the Party. Forman had just returned from a trip to Algeria, and had been in other countries of the Third World that had undergone a revolutionary process. He gave us the benefit of his investigation by introducing two very important concepts that became the backbone for the internal structuring of our national apparatus. The first was the 10-10-10 organizing concept; the second was the concept of how power could flow smoothly from a centralized High Command to the regional chapters.

The 10-10-10 is a very simple and effective system. I believe that Forman said he first learned of it in Sekou Touré's Republic of Guinea in Africa. We started by dividing L.A. into ten sections. Each of the ten sections would have a section leader. Then each major section would be divided into ten sub-sections. Each sub-section would have a sub-section leader. Thus far, you would have L.A. divided into one hundred sub-sections. Then we would divide the sub-sections, and make each rank and file Party member responsible for a certain number of blacks within a sub-section.

L.A. would be run by a central staff, which would be modeled along the lines of National Headquarters' Central Committee. The central staff of L.A. would usually communicate their commands through the ten section leaders, who would in turn relay them to the sub-section leaders. It was the job of the sub-section leaders to relay their commands to each Panther in the rank and file. Each member of the rank and file was responsible in the community.

In L.A., all commands that had to do with ideology,

only to the National Headquarters complex of San Francisco-Oakland chapters. Even now, the real stronghold of the Panthers is California, which is *Panther territory*.

strategy, and tactics, would come from the Central Committee of National Headquarters in Oakland to the L.A. Central Staff, which would be responsible for carrying them out through the 10-10-10 organizational setup.

Forman suggested that the Central Committee of National Headquarters in Oakland be known as the High Command. He considered the use of the term High Command important because of the military import that it carried. It would give the necessary psychological message to every Panther, particularly when the Party was geared to carry out the threat of *If Huey Goes the Sky's The Limit.*

Forman's concepts were first put into practice in L.A., and then as the Party spread into a national organization in the ensuing months, were used across the country. Because they were carried out so effectively, the Party became very efficient in disseminating its political propaganda through the black communities. In L.A. we could sell six thousand Panther newspapers in three days. *We were organized.*

To climax those fruitful five days of organizing, a meeting was arranged largely through intermediation by Forman, between the hierarchy of the Party and its complement in Ron Karenga's US. It was held at Karenga's headquarters, which is called *The Dahibu,* on Broadway—a few blocks down from the Black Congress. LeRoi Jones, who had recently arrived in town for poetry readings, was there. (It was the first time I had seen LeRoi since his escapades with the New Jersey courts, and he had lost so much weight in jail I hardly recognized him.) Although the coming together of the Party and US dealt with nothing of substance, it had a steadying effect in terms of the recent friction.

Things moved smoothly for the next two or three weeks that preceded the Oakland celebration on February 17th. As activities were being finalized in Oakland, we were doing the same in L.A. Our big day was to be the 18th, and various activities were also planned for the 19th and 20th.

A few days before the 17th, Stokely Carmichael came into

Oakland. Making the trip with him were SNCC people, Chico Neblett and Ethel Minor. Stokely had arrived early in order to be able to pay a visit to Huey—a visit that was well publicized by the news media.

Following right behind Stokely was Forman. With Carmichael and Forman in town at the same time a few very important strategic moves were made in those couple of days preceding the 17th. At that time the Central Committe was only a skeleton crew, consisting of Seale as Chairman, Newton as Minister of Defense, Cleaver as Minister of Information, and David Hilliard as National Headquarters Captain, a rank which actually made him responsible for the functioning of the rank and file when the organization grew to national proportions.* Not only was the leadership cadre underdeveloped, but the public image of the Party was still a distorted one, despite the national attention the Party had been receiving because of Huey's case. This image still remained military rather than political, and even more damaging, there was the tendency to try and write the Panthers off as "thugs" or "Kamikaze niggers." We did not have a national leader who was recognized outside of the small clique of the black and white left.

Huey was popular inside the leftist circles, but unfortunately his ideas had not received wide exposure before his imprisonment, and to the larger world he was more famous as a *"cause célèbre"* than an individual political leader. It was only later that Eldridge, because of his skills as a writer, was to give the Party a leader who could not be discounted as a leather-jacket-wearing "thug." (If those outside the leftist cliques would read some of Huey's writings from jail, they would discover a sensitive and intelligent analysis of our social and political ills; although they might find the solutions too harsh for their tastes.)

It was because the national and international image of the Party needed a new dimension that the High Command

---

* At that time, his position was reclassified Chief of Staff.

made the decision to add Stokely Carmichael, Rap Brown, and James Forman to its ranks. Eldridge announced the appointment of the new Panther officials on national television on the eve of Huey's Birthday Celebration. The timing was perfect.

Stokely was made Prime Minister. It was a job he could handle with facility because of his grace in moving in national and international political arenas. He presented the correct image of the Party inside the country and outside. It seemed only fitting that Rap Brown be Minister of Justice, since to many Afro-Americans he represents the individual *whipping boy* of America's grossly unjust system, and no one speaks about the struggle of Afro-Americans with more ferocity and frankness. James Forman was made Minister of Foreign Affairs. (With Cleaver and Forman, the Party would have two strong-willed, behind-the-scenes master-minds and theoreticians.) He also had vast international and national contacts, and was looked upon in serious circles as a man of wisdom, stability, and revolutionary resolve and discipline.

The Party also sprang the news on the eve of the 17th that the Panthers and SNCC had merged. Since, in fact, most people thought of SNCC in terms of its flamboyant personalities Carmichael, Brown and Forman—the concept of the merger had very little lasting effect on anybody outside of the two parties involved. When one of my old ladies heard Eldridge explain that Stokely, Rap, and Forman had been made Ministers in the Party, and that the Party was merging with SNCC, all she could compartmentalize in her brain was that "Stokely and Rap had joined the Party." She did not grasp the idea of the merger at all. In fact she made a chance remark about the Party taking over SNCC; which seemed a correct analysis to her, if Stokely and Rap had become Ministers.

The Party was only sixteen months old, and as recently as four months before, it had seemed doomed to obscurity with the loss of its co-founder and leader Huey Newton. And now by a miraculous change of fortune, it would bask in glory at the "celebration of the year" for the black liberation movement. It would announce there that it had courted and won the hand of three of the prized leaders in the black liberation movement, and that the established organization, SNCC, had decided to cast its lot with the Party it had only a short while ago considered immature and transitional, although necessary. *Who would be able to deny that the Black Panther Party had moved to the forefront of the black liberation movement?*

Unfortunately, around midnight on that same evening, enmity developed over whether SNCC and the Party were involved in a "merger," as Eldridge said, or a "coalition," as Forman defined it. The audience was not clued in on what was happening, and as Forman and Cleaver each expressed his interpretation of the relationship between the two organizations, they cheered just as wildly for each man.

It was that type of night in Oakland, on February 17th, 1968. Over five and a half thousand people, mostly militant blacks, filled the Oakland Auditorium to capacity—many wearing their Afro hairstyles and dressed in African styled shirts and dresses. They were emotionally charged for what was to prove an exciting evening.

Arrangements had been handled expertly by the Party. No police were allowed inside the auditorium by a mandate from the Party. The policing was done by the more than three hundred Panthers who were on hand. (We had to do some last-minute recruiting to beef up the ranks.) Most of the Party members were packing pistols, and had rifles easily accessible. This was a necessary precaution to guard against two possible eventualities: 1: the emotional electricity reaching such a peak that the affair would become uncontrollable and the trigger-happy Oakland police who were outside in droves would pour in on us; 2: an assassination attempt on one of the leaders who was present that night. As the crowd began to flow in, every man and woman was searched at the entrance by a Panther, from the tip of his toes to the top of his head, for anything that vaguely resembled a weapon. In the lobby outside the main hall of the auditorium, on the ground level and in the balcony, Panthers patrolled the aisles, watching for any disturbance or anything which might be suspicious.

The top brass of the Party, plus a selected entourage of brothers, arrived and entered the main hall from a side entrance, walking up onto the stage which was already set up. There were nine chairs on the stage; four to the left, and four to the right of a large African wicker chair which was imposing in its position in the middle.

Cleaver, Carmichael, Seale, Ron Dellums, who was a progressive black Berkeley City Councilman, Forman, Bunchy, Chico Neblett, and a surprise guest, Rap Brown, sat to the left and the right of the African wicker chair. Nobody sat in that chair—it was the one Huey had sat in when the now famous picture-poster of him holding the rifle and the spear had been taken. It was symbolically empty, hopefully to be filled upon Huey's rapid return to the Party leadership.

Rap's appearance at the birthday celebration was a welcome surprise. He had come into town to see his lawyer and had dropped by and come over with the Party.

The program was gotten under way by Bunchy reading the Invocation, which was the stirring poem by Claude McKay, *If We Must Die*. It seemed to me that those words never rang truer than that night. They seemed to leap off the paper and come driving home, until at the end of that beautiful short poem, I had to catch my breath:

> If we must die, O let us nobly die,
> So that our precious blood may not be shed
> In vain; then even the monsters we defy
> Shall be constrained to honor us though dead!
> O kinsmen! we must meet the common foe!
> Though far outnumbered, let us show us brave,
> And for their thousand blows deal one deathblow!
> What though before us lies the open grave?

Like men we'll face the murderous, cowardly pack,
Pressed to the wall, dying, but fighting back!

Seale, Carmichael, Dellums, Brown, and Forman spoke that evening. Cleaver was the Master of Ceremonies. Each speaker was inspirational, as if pushed to his oratorial limits by the speaker who preceded him. Rap and Stokely were particularly brilliant.

There were cries from the crowd of *Free Huey,* and *Happy Birthday Huey*. Because we were so close to the Oakland county jail, I couldn't help but think that Huey heard every cry loud and clear, although I know he couldn't. Judging from the frenzied shouts, which got louder and louder, other people must have felt the same way.

Putting the finishing touches to a magnificent evening was the popular soul group, The Impressions. They sang their hit tune of that time "We're A Winner," which summed up the way everybody felt that evening.

The next day, Sunday the 18th, the Party carried the celebration to L.A., and an afternoon affair at the L.A. Sports Arena. The audience was as large and as enthusiastic, as the one in Oakland.

Over a hundred Panther brothers had been brought down to L.A. The top brass flew by plane, but the overwhelming majority came in two huge buses the Party rented. It must have been impressive to black people at the Sports Arena that day to see Panthers walking around with their black leather jackets worn loosely draped across both shoulders—a style imitative of the leather-coated German officers of World War II.

The program at the Sports Arena was the same as the Oakland Auditorium, with a few exceptions. Dellums, who was a local participant, had been replaced by Ron Karenga. Also making the scene was Tijerina, the Mexican-American liberation leader from New Mexico whom the white press portrays as more notorious than Zapata. When he came on stage he grabbed Rap, then Stokely, and then Karenga, and gave each a big bear-hug. Providing the entertainment was the versatile Oscar Brown, Jr., and his beautiful sultry old lady, Miss Jean Pace.

The celebration at the Sports Arena redeemed all of our previous mistakes in trying to gain a foothold in L.A. We had *arrived* as far as all the people there on the 18th were concerned. The celebration was followed by two frantic days of organizing and fund raising, which covered the entire spectrum of L.A.'s black society.

After the three days in L.A., the Party went back to the San Francisco-Oakland area to do six more days of organizing and fund raising. We were trying to squeeze the most out of the time that Stokely and Forman had to spend on the west coast.

By the end of these nine days, a large sum of money had accumulated for Huey's defense and to keep the Party machinery moving. The Party had become the vanguard—an established organization.

But this flush of success was to be short-lived and ill-fated, for the major accomplishment would have been the merger of the Panthers and SNCC into a superstructure of unquestionable eminence. But this did not happen, and the enigma of this nine-day affair was the inability to decide whether there was a *merger* or *coalition* between the Party and SNCC. This troublesome issue kept cropping up, and five months later there was a controversial schism between SNCC and the Party. (This was in July, when high officials of the Party went to New York to bring Huey's case before the UN.) And even before that, Rap Brown resigned as Minister of Justice, and James Forman abdicated from his post as Minister of Foreign Affairs. This left only Stokely Carmichael as Prime Minister, which he was in name more than anything else.

As crippling to the results of the nine-day affair as the schism between SNCC and the Party was the more immediate action of the Oakland Police Department. Their timing couldn't have been better if it had been conceived in

Hollywood. Waiting until Carmichael, Forman, and Brown had all departed the west coast scene, and the emotional atmosphere had dropped from its stratospheric level, they began to make wholesale arrests of Panther members in the Bay area.

They started at the top. On Sunday morning of February 25, the Oakland police forcibly entered Chairman Bobby Seale's appartment in Oakland, and made a strong-arm arrest of him and his wife Ardie, at the point of a shotgun. I was shocked at their audacity in making the charge, *conspiracy to commit murder*. They were really freaking out.

Outside of Bobby's apartment that night they also busted the two officers from the L.A. chapter who were up at National Headquarters, Bunchy and his brother Glen. Busted along with them were National Headquarters Captain David Hilliard, and a sister named Audrey. They charged them with having illegal firearms under the seat of the car they were driving.

I instantly knew what was happening. The police were going into their "old bag of tricks," and bringing out the conspiracy game and the trumped-up charges routine to throw Party members in jail. That the charges would not hold water made no difference, because Bobby, Bunchy, David, Glen, Ardie, and Audrey had to be bailed out of jail —and that was very expensive. (None of the charges made that night against anybody were to hold up in court.)

There was nothing to do but sit tight and try to ride out the offensive. Before the Oakland police let up, they had arrested another dozen or more Panthers on assorted charges from using profane language to resisting arrest. They accomplished what they had set out to do, for in little more than a week, through bail fees, they had dried up the capital we had gained by nine days of fund raising and two months of planning.

| 7 |

As March 1968 came in, the High Command had again settled down to continuing to mount the Free Huey Movement. In addition to the National Headquarters complex of San Francisco Oakland, there was now the potentially formidable satellite of L.A.

We were busy trying to build the chapter in L.A. Not having our own office at the time, we used an office at the Black Congress, which was put at our disposal (a few months afterward we severed relations with the Black Congress and established our own office on Central Avenue and 43rd Street). Our first step was the recruitment of young black brothers and sisters into the Party.

Numbers were synonymous with power, or at least with popularity. Although I cannot remember hearing anybody talk specifically about it, I believe it was mainly for this reason that it was fairly easy to gain admittance to the Party in those days. We hoped to be able to reach the point where we could boast that we had more people than any other organization—even the Muslims, who have been the only other effective mass black organization of the '60's. This would be a sign that the Party had arrived as the most power organization.

In the spring of '68, particularly among the young blacks, the popularity of the Party was at such a high tide that however fast we processed the new recruits, there was still a steady flow of them into the L.A. chapter.

During that summer, when the Party had almost reached its full growth, I made a casual study of the age breakdown of the membership because it interested me that we were the first mass movement among blacks, to my knowledge, to have depended so heavily on the youth. (Neither Marcus Garvey's Back to Africa movement nor Elijah Muhammad's Muslim movement had the same emphasis upon young people.) I found that in '68, the ages of the top-ranking leadership in the party ranged from about twenty-six to thirty-four years. Huey was twenty-six then, Bobby, thirty-one, and Eldridge, thirty-four. The second level of leadership usually ranged in age from twenty-one to about twenty-six. This level of leadership included officials in chapters in places such as Seattle, New York, Newark, etc. It was bulwarked by Captains; each chapter in a city usually having from one to four Captains, and their authority being slightly less, but their responsibility just as great as the local ministry. Also included in this level were the section leaders, who were directly under the authority of the Captains.

The largest cluster of people in the Party were in the rank and file, and fell within the age range of sixteen to twenty-one. This was the life blood of the Party, the young black brothers and sisters who, until their potential was seen by Huey Newton and Bobby Seale, had for the most part been overlooked and snubbed by the organized black movement. And they were the most impressionable and most easily disciplined and directed.

In L.A. I found that there was a competitiveness, especially at the lower levels, for advancement within the ranks. It was healthy in the sense that a young brother or sister could work hard in his or her section, and because of that might catch the eye of the L.A. central staff and be promoted to a sub-section or a section leader. Of course, for this to happen, somebody of higher rank in the same section would have to be lagging and be in line for a demotion.

To have rank in the Party, and therefore authority, was something to strive, or to connive for. A Party member was justifiably proud of his rank, it being representative of a definite level of achievement; it even gained for him a modicum of attention in the world outside of the Party.

In L.A., and it was indicative of other chapters in the Party as well, brothers would address each other by their rank first, and then the given name (the calling of the rank was to show respect for authority, and using the given name afterwards showed brotherly familiarity). For example, a brother would address Tommy Lewis, who was one of the top young leaders in our chapter, as "Lieutenant Tommy."

The reference to a Party member by rank was practiced to an even greater degree when the top hierarchy was involved, whether local staff or national headquarters. A Party member would say "The Chairman" instead of Bobby Seale. Or he would say "The Minister of Defense" and not utter Huey's name.

In L.A., a Party member would say "The Deputy of Defense"—and you knew he was talking about Bunchy. At the level of the ministers, local and national, the dropping of the given name and the calling of the minister by rank alone was the deepest sign of respect. It was just accepted as gospel that every Party member knew who you were referring to.

This respect, which bordered on reverence, was an integral part of the Party's military style of organization and the psychological attitude that went with it. Although the Party from the beginning stated that it was political, most of its efforts in the first couple of years dealt with its military aspects.

If the Party had not first instituted military discipline in the period during the summer and fall of '68, when its membership soared to over two thousand, there would have been an almost uncontrollable situation. Each city chapter would have had its own enclave of power, thereby spawning indi-

Picking Up the Gun | 89

vidual leaders who would in effect have functioned as war-lords. Centralized authority would have broken down, and each chapter could have run its own political line, a situation which undoubtedly would have led to anarchism. Anarchism would have weakened the strength of the Party among the people by giving it a "wishy-washy, anything might happen" type of image.

From my own experience and observation I have come to believe that the establishment of military discipline (*i.e.*, the following of orders, adherence to a chain of command, train-ing in weaponry, etc.) should be the first consideration of any organization in the black liberation movement. It pro-vides a means of enforcement or at least a threat of enforce-ment (which is usually sufficient). It also keeps power and control in the hands of the leadership.

Our nucleus of young brothers in the L.A. chapter came from the Teen Post on Central Avenue where Bunchy worked. After joining, most of them told their friends, and they too began to flock down to our office at the Black Con-gress to sign up for the Party.

The processing was uncomplicated. There was a standard application form sent down from National Headquarters that we gave to each new recruit in L.A. He was to fill it out completely and turn it in to one of us on the local staff. Actu-ally, it was almost as routine as an application for an office job, until you came to a section which was headed by the question: *Have You Ever Been Arrested?* There was the usual slot for a "Yes" or "No" reply, and then a specific breakdown for the type of arrest: robbery, car theft, etc.

The Central Staff in Los Angeles had the power to decide who would be in or who would be refused membership in the Party. I can't remember anybody being refused member-ship in the early days of recruitment.

Young black activists used to express their alarm to me about the Party seemingly recruiting so loosely. I didn't share their paranoia about the possibility of there being heavy infiltration by the FBI or local police intelligence. I didn't think the "Man," as he is called, had the manpower to waste at that stage of the game, although I'm sure that once we became a threat in L.A., he probably slipped some people in on us. (It is important to note that Larry and Jean Powell, who testified before the Senate Investigating Committee in the spring of 1969 that the Panthers "murdered dissident members," were members in good standing. If they had been police informers *from the beginning,* they really fooled me, and I guess others too, for they had much responsibility.) But if any of those brothers we recruited in the early days in L.A. were the Man, I have to give credit to the FBI or L.A. police intelligence—because they're really recruiting brothers off the streets, or people who act so well that they should do it as a profession. Otherwise, it seems that the Man plays upon internal difficulties to induce those who are weak enough to become informers.

It took only one or two days to process the application of a new recruit. Then he would be contacted by telephone, or would be informed when he dropped by the office at the Black Congress that he was now a Panther. (At one time in Oakland, each new member was given a membership card with his name on it, signed by Bobby and Huey and the local captain. This procedure was never used in L.A.)

Because we had so much organizing to do in L.A. in the beginning, we had to leave the new recruits more or less to themselves during the new chapter's first weeks. Each member was given a mimeographed sheet with the names and positions of the High Command, and the Ten Point Program and October 1966 platform that had been put together by Newton and Seale.* They were told (and we meant it) that it was mandatory that they know by memory everything on that mimeographed sheet of paper. At general section meetings a few months later, any member might be asked at random to stand up before the group and recite the

---

* This Ten Point Program is commonly called, *What We Want.*

Ten Point Program. If someone didn't know it or was sloppy in his presentation, adjectives and cuss words describing the recruit's ignorance would flow freely from the authority in charge. He stood a chance of being called everything but the Son of God.

I knew brothers and sisters who missed meetings because they weren't sure of the Ten Point Program. I used to be able to recite it from memory letter-perfect. It was my ten commandments at one time, and I still believe it is a solid projection of objectives that Afro-Americans strive for.

The program went like this:

1. We want freedom. We want power to determine the destiny of our Black Community.
2. We want full employment for our people.
3. We want an end to the robbery by the white man of our black community.
4. We want decent housing, fit for shelter of human beings.
5. We want education for our people that exposes the true nature of this decadent American society.
   We want education that teaches us our true history and our role in the present day society.
6. We want all black men to be exempt from military service.
7. We want an immediate end to POLICE BRUTALITY and MURDER of black people.
8. We want freedom for all black men held in federal, state, county and city prisons and jails.
9. We want all black people when brought to trial to be tried in court by a jury of their peer group or people from their black communities, as defined by the Constitution of the United States.
10. We want land, bread, housing, education, clothing, justice and peace. And as our major

political objective, a United Nations-supervised plebiscite to be held throughout the black colony in which only black colonial subjects will be allowed to participate, for the purpose of determining the will of black people as to their national destiny.

In addition to learning the program and the hierarchy, every Panther was required to have his personal copy of Mao Tse-tung's little handbook for the Chinese people. Party members would study the "little red book" religiously. I could walk into our office at the Black Congress at any given time, and the brothers and sisters who were not involved at that moment in Party duties would be reading it.

This was not only true of the office. Usually, three or four Panthers would live together in an apartment or flat, and when they were home together there would be frequent discussions about the red book. In this way, the young brothers and sisters could keep their thoughts focused on revolutionary rhetoric (although at times, since they had not arrived at this rhetoric on their own, I thought the brothers and sisters had a tendency to be doctrinaire and dogmatic).

There were concepts in the red book which got more emphasis than others, such as the concept of criticism and self-criticism. This is a key concept—for to criticize a brother or sister is usually very difficult, because of the ultra-sensitive defensive mechanism which has been developed by black people as an adaptation for survival in a hostile world. (This defensive mechanism is an adaptation of the emotions in the same way that a reflex is an adaptation of the body. You can see it manifest itself in one form in the debate that almost invariably ensues if one black man seeks to give another some information. The less a person knows of a subject, the more such a debate borders on violence—as if for one brother to passively accept information from another would be submitting to a silent but definitive judgment on his ignorance.) For the most part, in the training of recruits, the critical and self-critical approach to getting along and solving problems showed *definite* results.

The uniform was the most visible part of the regular equipment of the Party. Every new recruit coming into the L.A. chapter was informed that he had to get the complete uniform of black leather jacket, black beret, and black pants. If he did not have enough money to get the leather jacket immediately, he was required to at least get the beret and pants.

We didn't have to prod the brothers or sisters. It was an "in" thing on the streets to have a real leather jacket, or if you couldn't raise enough change for that, at least a synthetic one. This was even before Bobby and Huey picked up on it as the Panther uniform. (This is, in fact, the reason that Huey gives for adopting black leather as the uniform for the Party at its inception. The beret, of course, has always been popular with revolutionary movements.) The young brothers and sisters were imitating the hustlers and pimps, who could afford and were wearing leathers. (The jacket became so highly identified with the Party in California that, although I had about four leathers, I was leery about wearing one when traveling the streets alone. A leather would make you a walking target. The "pigs" in L.A. or the Bay Area would try to whip you out of your leather if they caught you by yourself.)

Before the emergence of the Party uniform, the most popular dress of black organizations or individual black nationalists was the African dashiki. The dashiki was symbolic of the new identity, awareness of the African heritage, and the cultural ties with Africa. The dashiki was hated by the Party as being indicative of "jive ass" cultural nationalism.

If a Party member wore a dashiki, he was met with derisive looks and whisperings about being a cultural nationalist, the highest form of impiety for a Panther. In fact, in New York there was a faction of very good Panther brothers who had a real hang-up because they couldn't understand the Party's dislike of dashikis and cultural nationalism. I never really agreed with it myself, for it seems that the majority of black people are cultural nationalists at this time. And you can't deny the sincerity of brothers like LeRoi Jones or Fred Ahmed Evans and his people.

The most essential part of the standard equipment of a Party member was the *gun*. The gun had overnight capitulated the Party into the vanguard of the black liberation movement, thereby shoving the black liberation movement into a new era. *The era of the gun.*

As the gun was the key to the rise of the Party to the top of the heap but it was also to be its Achilles' heel. When the police thought of the Party, visions of young black brothers packing heavy caliber weapons must have danced through their imaginations. Once the image and reputation of the Party became known to them, they inevitably overreacted in any dealing with a Panther, however harmless the initial reason for the contact happened to be.

This was a reality the Party had to deal with. That is why in L.A. and in any Party chapter for that matter, a gun was essential for a new recruit. Because once he wore that black jacket, he also wore the Panther reputation as far as the police were concerned. And the police were going to treat him as a Panther regardless of what his actual Panther involvement was while a member, or what his intentions for joining were in the first place. That is why Panther officials were quick to warn new recruits that they had better know what they were getting into, because we were involved in a dangerous business.

In March '68 Huey issued an Executive Mandate from jail, which said that every Party member had to have enough firepower to protect his household. This mandate was issued after the pigs had arrogantly kicked in Eldridge's apartment door and ransacked his place in January '68, and kicked in Bobby Seale's door and tried to jack him up the next month.

There was automatic expulsion if this mandate was not followed. I had three high caliber pistols in my apartment. If you were a Party official, the mandate would be enforced more rigidly, because you were supposed to set a correct example for the rank and file.

Usually, it did not take more than a couple of weeks until a recruit was fully indoctrinated. Then the recruit, whether a brother or sister, was put into one of the ten sections in L.A., according to where he or she lived. From then on the recruit was the responsibility of his sub-section and section leader.

While we were busy getting ourselves together in L.A., the Party was making a move into the electoral political arena in northern California. The Peace and Freedom Party had been talked into putting up Huey as their candidate for Congressman in his Congressional district. I knew the PFP'ers up north must have balked becausse many of those in southern California wore puzzled looks. Granted, it was somewhat out of the ordinary to run a candidate who had no chance of serving a Congressional term if he was convicted and had to serve a prison sentence. (When we began to have meetings with the L.A. PFP chapters, I had to continually assuage the wounded feelings of some of their people who somehow felt that they had gone for the greasy pig.)

When PFP announced in March that Huey was a candidate for Congress and, following right on the heels of that, Bobby Seale's candidacy in Oakland's 17th Assembly District and Kathleen Cleaver's in San Francisco's 18th, my mind flashed back to the meeting in December in the big, run-down building not far from Market Street. I thought of that bespectacled white youth who had argued futilely that if the Party defined the politics of the black community, they would in effect be defining policy for the PFP. I was curious about what he was thinking this time!

It was a good move, however, for both the Party and PFP. It was good for PFP because they were publically espousing a position to the left of the Eugene McCarthy and Robert Kennedy camps, and stating that they were mainly interested in the issues rather than winning or losing individual races. When they nominated Huey, Bobby and Kathleen, nobody could say that they were lying. In terms of the Party, the entry into the electoral political arena gave more exposure to the Free Huey Movement and the political program of the Panthers.

One unfortunate development was the friction among the black candidates in the race. Kathleen was running against a black incumbent, Willie Brown, and Bobby was pitted against John George. There was vicious name-calling by the Party directed toward Brown and George, who were not the most radical of candidates. The spectacle of black leaders feuding at a petty level created bad vibrations in the black community. When I think back, I believe the Party lost more than it gained, for they sacrified their image in the community for token white radical support.

Somewhere around March 15th or 16th, after I had just returned from a trip to National Headquarters (it was not unusual for me to fly up there two or three times a week), I was walking down Arlington Boulevard in L.A. when I ran into Bunchy. He was on his way to his girlfriend's apartment. I had just been there looking for him, and Yvonne had told me only that Bunchy wasn't there. I don't remember her telling me anything else because I'm sure I would not have forgotten, but then she had no way of knowing what I did not know.

Bunchy asked me, "Did you hear about what happened to Glen?"

I told him I hadn't.

I saw a faraway look in his eyes, a look that I was to see in the eyes of Panthers many times in the future, and a look that people must have seen in my eyes many times. A look that says that there are no words to express the loss of a friend and a brother. A look that asks why did it have to be Glen, or Little Bobby, or Little Tommy?

Bunchy told me that Glen had been shot to death in Compton, California, a night or so ago. Nobody knew who the murderers were, except that they were supposed to be street hustlers. What actually went down was unclear, but Glen seemed to have walked into a trap. He had told a few people that he was leery about going out to Compton for what was supposedly a harmless rendezvous.

Glen had taken two of his assailants with him, if this was any consolation. Bunchy told me that he had seen him at the wake the night before, and that he had a very peaceful look on his face.

"It's good that he didn't suffer."

"Yeah," Bunchy said.

We walked back to Yvonne's apartment and got high that day. The LAPD never did catch the men who shot Glen to death. I don't know, maybe they felt that someone had done them a favor in disguise by killing a Panther, and one who was an official in the L.A. chapter at that. The L.A. chapter set up an armed guard around Bunchy's apartment to make sure that nobody tried to down him.

Glen's funeral was on March 18th. It was the first funeral of a Panther member. Bunchy and Yvonne came over to pick me up, and together we rode over to the funeral home which was on Figueroa Drive. A delegation of twenty to thirty Panthers had come down for the funeral, including Bobby Seale, Bobby Hutton, and a Panther official from Marin City who had been in the joint with Eldridge and Bunchy, who was called "Baby Dee."

It was a very touching funeral. A few of the Panther sisters broke down and cried uncontrollably, and the only thing that held my tears in check, and probably those of the other brothers who had known him, was that it would be looked upon as somewhat unmasculine to be so free with your emotions. *I had really dug Glen as a person.* He was more mature than most of the other brothers in the chapter, being about twenty-six or twenty-seven, and we had gotten into some deep and beautiful conversations about women, jazz, life, and other things.

At the conclusion of the funeral, everybody walked single

file to the casket for a final look at the body. Glen was resting very peacefully, and I thought as I looked down upon his body that this was the first person I had really grown to know, and feel somewhat close to, who had died in his youth, and died tragically. It was frightening. (In the next few months, the death of a comrade was to become a more and more common experience and I became accustomed to living with the possibility of my own early death.)

After the funeral I borrowed a car and drove Bobby Seale and Little Bobby Hutton to the L.A. International Airport. The Chairman had to get back to Oakland for a court appearance which was scheduled for that afternoon (he was later convicted on a charge of being too close to a police station with a shotgun that had a barrel over the legal size, and was put on probation). Although I didn't know it then, it was to be the last time I would see and talk to Little Bobby Hutton.

Before the impact of Glen's death had lessened, the California police opened what must have been their spring offensive on the Party. They zeroed in on National Headquarters in Oakland.

National Headquarters had been holding their general meetings at St. Augustine Episcopal Church, where Father Earl Neil was the minister. (Father Neil was the spiritual advisor to the Party and also to Huey.) On April 3, during one of these meetings, twelve Oakland pigs—accompanied by two men of the cloth (a white Catholic priest and a black clergyman)—kicked in the door and armed with 12 guage shotguns invaded the church.

Leading the Oakland cops was a Captain McCarthy, who three days later was to figure prominently in the first shooting flare-up between the Party and the police since the night of October 28.

The pigs looked around and seemed puzzled about what to do once they got in. The word came down to us in L.A. that they made queries about Bobby Seale's whereabouts, since

Bobby had left the meeting a few minutes earlier and had put another Panther official in charge. The pigs left shortly after entering, without making any arrests, and we could only surmise that Bobby, who was to be the big catch—the purpose of this safari—had eluded them (around that time Bobby was constantly being harassed and there seemed to be a concerted effort to jack him up with some charge and take him off the streets again).

The next day, April 4, Father Neil called a press conference, where he vented his rage at the high-handed activities of the Oakland police. Any other day a press conference called by a man of the cloth assailing the police for their treatment of Panthers would have been front-page, or close to front-page, news. But not on April 4, for another man of the cloth, Martin Luther King, Jr., was felled that day by a hail of assassin's bullets in Memphis, Tennessee. A murder that chilled the country and the world.

8

The tragic assassination of Martin Luther King, Jr., seemed to push forward the time of the coming of the apocalypse that I, and most other black militant comrades, had been talking about since 1966. At no other time, except possibly during the summer of '67, was I more sure that we were going to take it to this mad dog, racist America, and that our struggle would end either in total victory or total defeat.

I know that when I heard the news it seemed to me that it could not be true—although during the few years preceding Dr. King's death, my comrades and I in moments of frustration over the stumbling block to our longed-for revolution that Dr. King had unwittingly allowed himself to become, would say that *"if the man was dead, it would speed up time."*

But when these words which were uttered without any real malice became an *unwanted* reality on April 4, I realized that I was very sorry for Dr. King—not because I naively felt that he was "too good to be killed," as I heard others say, for I thought that Malcolm X was the best of men and he was killed—but more because it was ironical that the man who played the role of the lamb would be butchered, while those of us who were playing the role of lions went unmolested.

Anybody would have though that Stokely or Rap, or anybody cut from that mold, would have gotten it first. But then, I should have realized Dr. King had made himself too big a target.

On that fourth of April, everything inside of me seemed to vibrate with the feeling that this was it. *That it was on.* In the two years that we had been talking *shit* to the white man we had been building up courage for the fight, and now we had the fight whether we *really* wanted it or not.

King's assassination gave us the perfect excuse to put the torch to America and let it burn. And, more important, people everywhere, on the four corners of the earth, were expecting us to do just that.

In L.A., Bunchy and myself and two or three other brothers in the leadership of the chapter immediately got together over at Bunchy's apartment. It was going to be necessary that we get together on just what we were going to do, because everybody thought the next twenty-four hours would bring forth a holocaust in the city.

Everybody in that room said it, but in different ways, about how they had waited and figured that something would move Dr. King out of our way. That he had been holding back the struggle. This had to be the only logical extension of any violent black militant's political philosophy. But what Dr. King's death meant to each of us in that room personally I don't know, for nobody talked of it. *I felt guilty that I had entertained such ominous thoughts.*

Nobody seemed to talk much about anything that day. I guess each one in his own way was paying a silent tribute to a man who was in his own style a true warrior for revolution in America. Whatever you thought of his beliefs, you then had to think about whether you would be willing to put yourself in the position to sacrifice *for your beliefs* what he did for his.

Hour after hour we watched TV—the scenes preceding Dr. King's murder at the motel in Memphis, his life before the movement, and his progress in the movement from the

Montgomery days of '55. The phone was constantly ringing. People were expressing their shock and searching for an inside clue as to what was in store for the next crucial days.

Many people dropped by the apartment that night. Most of them were militant black comrades, like Hakin Jamal, who is the cousin of Malcolm X. Everybody seemed to want to keep in touch with everybody else, and especially the Party, because everybody sensed the blood instinct that day.

The thing that preoccupied my mind, and I know everybody else's, was what were we going to do? We knew that the L.A. police had Bunchy's place, my place, the Panther headquarters and other places the Panther leadership frequented, under surveillance.

We all knew that they were waiting for us to move. I felt somewhat helpless because I knew that the police in L.A., as was the case around the country, had "one-upped us." They knew that the emotionalism in the black communities would be running high with Dr. King's death, and they were ready. As LeRoi Jones later said to me in an interview, "Emotionalism and light weapons ain't gonna beat this devil."

I didn't think then, and on reflection I don't think now, that the Party or L.A.'s black population in general had the troops or weapons to deal with the L.A. police in open street warfare. And that was the way L.A.'s black population would have geared the fight. Other people in the L.A. chapter leadership thought nearly the same.

Another Watts '65 type of scene would have been a bloodbath for black people. At best, it would have been a Pyrrhic victory.

As night began to fall on L.A. on the 4th, we in the Party leadership were on the spot. Many of the young brothers wanted to deal. Even if we could hold them in check until we could get a clearer picture of what was happening, if the black brothers and sisters outside of the organization broke loose, it would almost surely force our hand.

L.A. was tense, but nothing on a major scale broke loose on the 4th. By the next day, the 5th, the High Command had analyzed the situation and decided on a unified course of action. The orders flowed down to us to try and keep black people off the streets, to avoid the bloodbath that was surely in store for them. Actually, this decision was in line with a Party policy which had been in effect since the beginning—that insurrections were not a revolutionary tactic, for in a confrontation, the agents of the enemy, the police and national guard, have the advantage over black people.

We passed the word along to the section leaders to start walking and talking in the streets, explaining to the brothers and sisters that this was not the time or the way to stage an effective rebellion against racist America and her racist province of L.A. They would be shot down like dogs in the streets.

While we were out pounding the streets, telling the brothers and sisters to *hang loose,* up in the National Headquarters complex of San Francisco-Oakland they were doing the same thing.

The Black Congress was also out in the streets of L.A. telling black brothers and sisters to be *cool*—but for reasons which seemed, at least on the suurface, to be much different than our reasons. It was reported in the *Los Angeles Times* a week later that the leaders within the Black Congress had sat down with Police Chief Thomas Redding and worked out a deal. (This deal sealed our decision to leave the Black Congress building as soon as we were on our feet and able to rent an office.*)

Our people kept stressing the fact that we were not against burning "the motherfucker" to the ground. But it was not a correct revolutionary tactic at that time. The correct way of dealing with the L.A. power structure was to go in groups of twos and threes, sniping at policemen in squad cars, or dynamiting police stations. Or any action that would catch the enemy when his guard was down.

---

* We accomplished this about a month later.

L.A. hung loose on the fifth and sixth. So did Oakland and San Francisco. Washington, D.C. burned. Chicago burned.

It was about six o'clock in the morning of the seventh when the phone rang at my apartment and awakened me. At the other end was Bernice Scarborough, a chick that I used to go around with in Oakland. She was calling from there.

After an exchange of greetings, she went right to the point.

"Earl, have you heard the radio?"

"No, baby, what's happening?" I was still sleepy, and hoped that it was something important that caused her to wake me.

It was!

"They killed Bobby, and Eldridge is seriously hurt." Her voice was trembling as if she was afraid to tell me.

I was numbed. Everything went blank.

"When?" I asked. And I don't remember hearing the words come out of my mouth or even opening my mouth to say them. But I must have, because the silence at the other end of the phone was broken by an answer.

"It was on the radio this morning. They said it was a shoot-out with the Oakland police last night."

"Thanks, baby, I'll talk to you," I said, and put the phone back into its cradle. I didn't want to talk any more.

I didn't realize until much later that I hadn't asked Bernice which Bobby had been killed. The cops had been hounding Eldridge and Bobby Seale so much in the last few months that I just knew it had been Bobby Seale (when I found out a few hours later that it was Little Bobby Hutton who had been snuffed it did nothing to deaden the impact or change that sick feeling I had in the pit of my stomach).

For an hour or so I did nothing but sit, thinking some, but mostly just letting my mind wander. I did not really want to think about it. Bunchy called and said he and a brother called J.J. were coming over.

When Bunchy got to my apartment, he began to fill me in

on some of the details he had picked up. He had talked to Kathleen Cleaver.

It seems that Eldridge and Little Bobby Hutton had been forced into a house on 28th Street in Oakland (we later called it the Battle of 28th Street), after a patrol car with two policemen inside had opened fire on them. There was then a gunfight between Little Bobby and Eldridge and about fifty Oakland cops (the original two had called for reinforcements, who arrived what seemed like only seconds after the whole thing started).

The tear gas forced Little Bobby and Eldridge to take their chances on the outside with the police. They called out that they were going to surrender, and threw out a rifle. They came out, and Little Bobby was holding Eldridge who had been hit in the leg with a tear gas cannister.

One of the cops pushed Little Bobby away from Eldridge, and told Little Bobby to run toward a squad car which had a door open. Little Bobby ran with his hands in the air, and they opened fire and blew him into eternity.

They murdered him. A crowd of black people had gathered to watch the gunfight. With their own eyes they saw Little Bobby cruelly baited into running, so he could be shot in the back like an animal after the valiant fight he had put up for ninety minutes to save his life. The black people at the scene vigorously condemned the Oakland police with their shouts of "Murderers, murderers."

I believe to this day that the outcry against the cold-blooded murder of Little Bobby is what spared Eldridge's life. (The Oakland police later lied that they thought Little Bobby had a concealed weapon. Eldridge had thought ahead that they might try to set them up that way, so he tried to convince Little Bobby to take off all his clothes. Little Bobby, who was only seventeen, was too modest. Eldridge came out of that house as naked as the day he came into this world.)

Bunchy didn't have any information about who else in the Party was involved or how it actually got started.

I had really loved Little Bobby; I think everybody in the Party did. And I probably felt closer to Eldridge as a person than I did anyone else in the Party. But I knew on that day of the 7th that Bobby's murder and the wounding of Eldridge left no time for mourning, for they would not have wanted that. It was time for us to rededicate our efforts to what all of us considered important.

From that day on we were into a whole new thing. Another dimension. The reality of what Little Bobby's death meant to us as a Party sank in when I saw the grim but determined looks on the faces of Party members that day at our office in the Black Congress.

About three days later I went up to San Francisco. The events of the night of the sixth were beginning to be pieced together, and a clearer picture was emerging.

There had been three carloads of Panthers out that night in Oakland, going about picking up potatoes to make the potato salad for the Sunday barbecue and Free Huey rally the next day at Derfermery Park in Oakland. Eldridge and Little Bobby were in the middle car. The brothers were packing, but that was not unusual; the Party was under heavy police surveillance at the time because of the fear of us starting trouble in Oakland after Dr. King's death (we packed guns in L.A. for the same reason— it was just common sense).

The cars had stopped, and Eldridge had gotten out to take a piss. Eldridge said the next thing he knew, a police squad car with two cops inside had pulled up and ordered him to come around in front of their car. He had hesitated, trying to finish the business he had started, and a split second later a gun exploded in his face. (The cops say that they were ambushed, but nobody can explain how over fifty cops could assemble in less than two minutes. It seems impossible, unless you had cooked up a little scheme ahead of time and the first cop car was a decoy.)

At the crack of the gun, Eldridge hit the ground and yelled for the brothers to scatter. He got up and ran into the basement of a house. Little Bobby had followed him. That is when the gunfight started.

Warren Wells (a brother we called Killer Wells) was shot in the rear end as he tried to go for cover. One group of cops searched the area, while their cohorts were engaged in the gunfight, and flushed out and arrested six Panthers on charges of attempted murder. Three cops were wounded in the gun battle.

After Eldridge and Little Bobby surrendered, and they had murdered Little Bobby, they whisked Eldridge to Oakland's Highland Hospital and then to Vacaville State Penitentiary under machine-gun guard. Vacaville is heavy security, and if it had not been for our lawyers we would not have known what had happened, or what was happening.

They had revoked Eldridge's parole. We couldn't get him out.

The Party was busy trying to raise the bail during that week to get out the other seven brothers who were being held. The bail was fantastically high. It was so impossible that David Hilliard sent word out to the Party to leave him in until they lowered it.

One of the reasons, however, that made it an immediate necessity to free the seven brothers on bail was the harassment that they were going through. The Bay Area papers were running stories that all the Panthers had confessed that Eldridge was the one responsible for the shoot-out.

The Party lawyers, to discredit this attempt to show Party members as disloyal finks, got their own notarized statements from the brothers. They were later used as part of a federal civil suit against the City of Oakland.

Warren Wells: *". . . They told me that if I did not co-operate with them and give them the statement that they wanted, they had the power to see that Eldridge Cleaver and I would be convicted of the murder of Bobby Hutton and that we would both be sent to the gas chamber. . . . The officers took the statement, wrote it themselves, and then asked me to sign it, without letting me read it and without reading it back to me."*

Wendell Wade: ". . . *He then asked me what kind of gun I had, and then he pulled out a snub-nosed pistol and asked if the gun I had was loaded and would shoot, and said 'my gun can shoot, too.' During all this, he was pointing the gun right in my face.*"

Donnell Lanksford: ". . . *He then told me that Eldridge Cleaver had said that everybody had made statements against him, and so he was going to make statements against the rest of us. He also said that he already knew everybody who was involved and that he really didn't need any answers because he already knew anyway. But he said things would go very hard for me if I didn't give him the answers he wanted. He then asked me whether I was getting paid by the Black Panthers and said that nobody was getting any money except Eldridge Cleaver, Bobby Seale and Huey Newton. He said the lawyers were only going to do work for those three who had the money and wouldn't do anything for the rest of us. He told me also that if I told any of the things he said to me to my lawyer, he would deny them.*"

David Hilliard: " . . .*The officer told me I was a fool because it would only be bad for me to take the Fifth Amendment when I could answer yes or no. Then I requested a phone call to my attorney. He said I couldn't call an attorney until he gets ready for me to call an attorney. Then he said I had been looking at television too much if I thought I had a right to call an attorney.*"

Charles Bursey: ". . . *Sergeant Stevenson said, 'Eldridge Cleaver, that son-of-a-bitch, is no damn good and is just trying to bring everybody down with him because he knows he has no hope.' . . . They also told me that if I wouldn't make a written statement I could just make an oral statement as long as I said that Eldridge Cleaver started everything and was to blame for everything . . .*

"*When I was first arrested in a house in Oakland . . . the policeman who arrested me kicked me and told me that they should make me run out into the backyard, and he said, 'Yes, I should shoot you down with your own gun.' I was* *frightened and didn't know what he meant because I did not have a gun. They took off my shoes there and kicked me so hard that I still have a large bruise . . . [later] in the room they had taken me, two plainclothesmen were there and one told me if I didn't make a statement, they would beat me to within an inch of my life. He wrote out a thing similar to what I had told him previously at the house where I was arrested, but he told me that I had to add that I lost my shoes because they were two sizes too big for me while I was running . . ."**

I believe Killer Wells was the first Panther the Party got free. The day that Killer was let out, he and a group of us were standing talking in front of the San Francisco apartment of a Panther Field Marshal whom we called D.C. Three young black boys (they must have been about ten years old) were getting ready to play a shoot-'em-up game. Like we used to play cowboys and Indians, or cops and robbers. But their heroes were not Roy Rogers or the Lone Ranger.

One of the children said, "I'm gonna be Bobby Hutton." "I'll be Eldridge Cleaver," said a playmate. The third chimed in, "Okay, then I'm Huey Newton."

Everyone of us in that group standing there, smiled. I thought that nothing would be in vain, as long as it became part of a legacy to be inherited by generation after generation of young, committed Afro-American warriors. I knew that young warriors, cast in the image of the Bobby Huttons of times gone by and the times to come, would continue to regenerate themselves in America—like life inside the warmth of a diseased area.

The funeral is an event of the first magnitude in the black community. Because of the torture of day-to-day existence,

---

* All statements part of federal suit of Panthers *vs.* City of Oakland filed by C. Garry.

and the aura of death and decay around the lives of black people, the funeral becomes the symbolic occasion when the black man or woman is released from this prison on earth to something that has to be better.

Little Bobby's funeral was on April 13, 1968 at Ephesiams Church of God in Christ in Berkeley, California.

I have been to many funerals, but none that matched Little Bobby's in splendor and solemn significance. It was the first of what was to become a Panther tradition, a *Panther-style* funeral.

Nothing can match the first, unless it's the last.

At the funeral that day there were over two thousand people. Many friends of the Party from around the country had come to pay their condolences personally.

There were over three hundred Panthers, dressed splendidly in Panther uniforms, at the funeral. Before the ceremony they stood inspection for Chairman Bobby and the national and local officials. During the services, they lined the walls of the church. The eight pallbearers for Little Bobby were all members of the Party.

The first row of the church, to the left of the center, was reserved for the seating of national and local officials (this practice was followed in all Panther funerals, in whatever city they happened to be).

Chairman Bobby read a tribute to Little Bobby from Huey. (Little Bobby was the first to be able to boast, *I walked with Huey.*) Then Father Neil spoke very beautifully. But the most poignant address, judging from the emotional response, was delivered by Reverend E. E. Cleveland.

Reverend Cleveland told a story of "a man who was wandering in the desert, without water. He was coming close to death, by reason of thirst, when he stumbled upon a stream of water in the desert. This wanderer fell to his knees beside the stream, but found the stream muddy and almost undrinkable.

"From the other direction in the desert approached a fellow wanderer. When he came to the stream, the thirsty wanderer asked him why was the stream dirty . . . that he wanted a drink of clear water.

" 'The stream starts at the top of the mountain,' the wanderer told the thirsting man. 'And I have been to the top of the mountain. And at the top of the mountain where the stream begins, there is a pig in the stream. In order to make the stream clear, we must get that pig out of the stream.' "

The analogy with the police who were first called pigs by the Panthers, rocked the church with a tremendous response.

The interment for Little Bobby was at Mountain View Cemetery in Oakland. After the funeral services, a memorial tribute was held at Lake Merritt Park in Oakland, where a host of national and local Party leaders spoke.

At the memorial, Marlon Brando, also spoke of his sense of bereavement at Bobby's loss. Little Bobby had met Marlon about a week before his death when the actor had come to Eldridge's apartment as a guest of the Party. (At the time, he was doing research for "Quemada," a forthcoming film of his about a Third World liberation struggle.) Hakin Jamal, who, as I have mentioned, is the cousin of Malcolm X, had introduced Marlon to the Party.

We felt that Brando was sincere in his interest in the Party. In conversations with us he sought to analyze the destiny and plight of oppressed people, and what should be done about that oppression. After the funeral, he made several TV appearances where he made it known that he was sympathetic to the Panther movement.

The Party really began to tighten up after Little Bobby's death, and Eldridge (whom I called "El-Rage" after the night of the shoot-out) was in the joint. I never thought Eldridge's feet would hit the pavement again. (I would say to myself, if he can spin around and come up landing on his feet on this one, I'll have to give the brother credit. For he will have walked on water.)

It was in the next few months that the Party established

many of its major chapters in cities outside of California, New York included. Most of the credit goes to Chairman Bobby and Chief of Staff David, who were really on the run at that time, starting to build the national apparatus.

The job was made easier by the receptiveness to the Party of militant young blacks in ghettoes across America. They provided a plentiful crop of talented state and local leadership.

One example of this talented new leadership was a brother who was originally from Oakland and then went to the concrete jungle of New York where it is gospel that nobody and no organization has been able to follow Malcolm. He was Captain Pennywell. In a little over two months, after the Party started in New York, Pennywell had over four hundred brothers and sisters in the ranks.

In L.A. we intensified our efforts on all levels. One aspect of this was that we began to solidify our relationship with the L.A. Peace and Freedom chapters, so that we would have a viable physical and financial base in the white community.

I had met Marilyn Feldman, the wife of the jazz pianist Victor Feldman, on a plane trip back from San Francisco to L.A. She was a very nice person and was getting her feet wet in radical politics. She promised to organize neighborhood Peace and Freedom meetings for the Party and she began to do it regularly. There were also PFP neighborhood meetings organized through their local staff, but for the most part they were inefficient and chaotic.

During that spring of '68, from April to almost July, I was speaking two or three times a week to different neighborhood chapters of the PFP (I never knew L.A. had so many neighborhoods). The format of those meetings became standard. They were almost always held at the middle class suburban home of a Caucasian family. The attendance at these neighborhood meetings ranged from forty to a hundred people, and usually they were mingling socially when we arrived. I would show up with six to ten Panther brothers and our arrival, of course, would interrupt whatever social amenities were going on, as the middle class PFP'ers curiously watched the honored guests. (The first neighborhood meeting that we attended was at the home of the actress Barbara Nash. Marilyn Feldman had arranged it. On the flyer announcing this meeting was, "Guess Who's Coming to Dinner?—The Black Panthers!" Dig where that was at.)

After a short introduction by our host or our sponsor, I would get right into the presentation. The stone-faced Panther brothers would be stationed around the room, and to my side and rear at a military alert position. (Actually, there was no real danger at a meeting of this type, but it added a certain amount of dramatic flair.)

I would explain the beginnings of the Black Panther Party and why we felt our Ten-Point October platform was valid. Then I would proceed to point out the rare leadership qualities in Huey Newton and Eldridge Cleaver, and why the death of Little Bobby Hutton had turned a page on organized revolutionary activity in America in '68.

They would listen attentively. In fact, many of them were really caught up in what I was saying, not how I said it, or because I was saying it, but because any Panther spending an hour or so to talk to them provided an emotional and intellectual catharsis. *They had done their part in the revolution by coming to listen to a revolutionary.*

After the presentation, I would make a fund-raising pitch, and we would pass around a collection plate.

A lot of interesting little games used to be played at those meetings. When I think back, I always remember how the white women would stare at me while I was speaking (and at the other brothers who were bodyguarding; we often compared notes after a meeting). It was the type of stare which implies sexual invitation. At each meeting, there would be three or four of these white chicks who would prop their legs up in such a position that their skirts would recede up their thighs, and I had a clear visual shot to what they considered the essence of their power.

You had to be very strong to keep your mind on what you

had come there for. One time one of our captains summed it up perfectly. He said to me at one of these PFP meetings, "Brother, let's get out of this meeting. These white bitches are trying to put pussy on the brothers' minds."

Then there were the informal talk sessions after the formal presentations. I must have been asked a thousand times, "Are the Panthers intending to spread their armed warfare outside of the black community?" and I have repeated a thousand times, that "the Party does not intend to indiscriminately attack people. We are not racists who intend to terrorize the white community. However, we are committed to defending our own black communities."

That soothed their feelings. I have found, through talking to many white audiences on many different levels, that they are more interested in their individual plights at this point in time than in the plight of the white race. On this point, at this time, we have them beat.

| 9 |

One day in the early part of June, Bunchy called and told me that there would be a meeting at his house at midnight. This in itself was nothing unusual because we always held staff meetings that late, or later, after we had finished a day's work in the L.A. community.

When I arrived at Bunchy's house that night and knocked on the door, Captain Shermont Banks let me in almost immediately, as if they had been waiting for me to show up.

"Hey, what's happening," he said.

"Black folks," I replied.

Banks smiled. It was a type of sneaky smile, and it should have put me on my guard that there was something underhanded going on. Banks was one of the hardest working brothers in the Party, *but whatever else he was, a congenial brother he was not,* and he very rarely smiled at anything.

Banks returned to his seat, his chair being nearest to the door and making up one end of a semicircle. There was a couch and four brothers were sitting on it. They were members of our Elite Squad, which later became known as the Black Guard.

At the other end of the semicircle, with his legs crossed, sitting back playing with his heavy black mustache, was

Bunchy. (I thought to myself when I looked at Bunchy, "This nigger really looks like the devil." Bunchy had that heavy mustache, and being dark complexioned, he had a type of evil, sinister good looks, like the stereotyped slick, good-looking heavy in the movies.)

When I looked at Bunchy, I knew something was up.

"What's happening, nigger?" I said, trying to get some reaction from him so that I could see what he was about. (I knew Bunchy better than anyone else in the L.A. chapter. The two of us were at the top of the leadership, and we spent a lot of time together socially and politically. We also made many trips to San Francisco, both staying at Eldridge's.)

"Nuthin," Bunchy replied in a quick, gruff way that indicated there was not going to be any small talk that night.

Conveniently, there was one chair empty in the room. It faced the couch where the four brothers sat, and it would give Banks and Bunchy a profile view of its occupant (who would have to turn to look at Banks or Bunchy).

This had to be my seat, and as I sat, I made a mental note to myself; "You had better be at your sharpest tonight, because you're about to be put on trial."

I was on trial, and the six brothers in the room comprised the kangaroo court. I noticed they were all packing, which in itself was not uncommon (I was packing, too), but considering the situation it had a particular meaning. I quickly glanced at the faces around the room, and I instantly knew that they had me jacked sky-high. Banks had a smirk on his face—he never really dug me and the feeling was mutual.

Bunchy was still looking sinister, playing with his mustache. It was obvious that the whole thing was his idea, and he was determined to play to the hilt his role as the judge of this outlaw court.

I must admit that when I realized what was going down, my heart sank to the tip of my toes. I'm glad that they spoke first, after the initial exchange, because I wouldn't have been able to muster enough inside of me to bring forth words that would have sounded the least bit convincing.

"Brother Earl, we've been talking about your participation in the Party, and everybody here seems to feel that you're not doing enough," Bunchy started.

He had stood up, and was pacing to and fro, between where I sat and his chair. He never looked at me.

I leaned forward in my seat, spread my legs far apart, and cupped both my hands to my mouth, both to give the appearance of serious consideration to what was being said (which I *was* giving), and to be in a position where my eyes would be downward, to avoid their eyes, which I knew would be looking into mine to see signs of their triumph—*which they knew they had,* simply because in our world might made right. I didn't want the brothers to be able to gloat in their victory.

Bunchy was continuing. "Now, with your education, we feel that you could be doing more than you are." (I have felt many times that having an education is a yoke around my neck in the day-to-day, individual-to-individual dealings in the organized struggle. It makes you constantly suspect because many brothers feel that there is no reason for a person with an education to be involved. Of course, with time and proven service you can ride these feelings of suspicion out.)

"What you're saying can be looked at from two sides, Brother Bunchy. I disagree with you, Brother. But if you want to, we can examine what I've been doing and what you think I should be doing." I sallied forth with my attack, hoping to change the tide of the evening before Bunchy and his court got a foothold and really started getting off into my ass.

"Look, nigger you're always trying to be cute—we ain't gonna have that shit tonight," Bunchy cut in, and the effect of my attack, if it might have had any, was wiped out so completely that it took the wind out of me.

I leaned back in the chair. *An appeal to reason would have gotten absolutely nowhere in that room that night.*

Another brother, whose name was Lionel, took a turn. "Brother Earl (at times like this the term *brother* is an insult), you have been with the Party almost from the beginning. Although you have done a lot in L.A., we think you could be doing much more."

"Instead of doing that KPFK radio show and speaking at these college campuses," Bunchy picked up the attack (I was doing a fifteen-minute opinion show each Friday for KPFK FM in L.A., expressing Party views, and had been speaking at Free Huey rallies on the campuses in southern California; UCLA, Cal State, etc.) , "you should be giving political education classes to the ranks."

I knew *that* was correct. All of us in L.A.'s leadership had been talking about instituting political education classes. I probably should have put my time into those and pushed the other things aside. But I was not the only one lagging, and I refused to totally accept the blame.

Reluctantly, so far I had to agree that they had made points. But the next argument they presented, which was the thrust, made me discount everything they had said before.

"Now, you're making $700 a month as a consultant for that Watts Happening Coffee House (when I had returned to L.A. I was flat broke and took a job as consultant for Watts Happening because it was one of those poverty jobs where you could integrate making money with organizing. The twist to this was that Bunchy and most of the brothers were also working on poverty jobs. I quit that job in the next two weeks, although nobody else quit theirs) , and we feel that since you've been working three months, you owe us $2,100."

"You have got to be jiving," I said, and I had to smile, because of the obvious way they were putting me up against the wall.

"Nigger, we're not jiving," Bunchy said, "and we're giving you twenty-four hours to either give it up or get out."

As I looked at the faces in that room, I knew that I had been caught in the middle of a power play, which I gathered had developed because of a personality clash between Bunchy and myself. Bunchy had the power, having control of the army, and he had probably decided in his way that I was being *politically ambitious,* and he was going to move me out (I don't think anybody considered whether my actions, whatever they thought of them personally, were helping the Party or not).

I was given a bullet, a dumdum bullet, as a souvenir of that evening.

I left, and I was plenty shook up. They had really put me up against the wall. I stayed awake all night thinking.

I knew what the game was. I had to use my head and think, because if I didn't come up with something better than what they had put on me, they would have forced me right out of the Party.

I did a lot of thinking that night. One thought kept nagging me. "It sure is different when you are on the wrong end of the threat." I replayed all the power plays I had directly or indirectly participated in since the days at the Black House, and the running feud with the cultural nationalists. (I believe firmly—in fact I'm dogmatic in this belief—that these internal and external organizational power plays are like a malignant cancer eating away at the body of the black liberation movement.)

I quickly threw aside the idea of trying to organize a counter-force inside the ranks. That would be divisive; anyway, I didn't have the time. I decided that I would have to take my case to the highest body in the Party, the High Command. I was committed to the Party, and I wasn't dropping out.

I caught the first thing smoking out of L.A., a 7 A.M. PSA flight to San Francisco. When I got there, I went to the man I knew had the power to make things right—Eldridge. Eldridge had just been released from Vacaville a few days before.*

After Eldridge and I talked things out, he appointed me

---

* He had served fifty days. Judge Raymond Sherwin of Solano County had issued the orders to cut him loose, stating that he had been imprisoned illegally because of political reasons.

Deputy Minister of Information (the second deputy to be appointed to the Party, the first having been Bunchy). I deeply respect Eldridge for what he did for Huey, and in developing the Party, and on another level I appreciate in a very personal way the things he did for me in my development and rise within the ranks of the organization.

I returned to L.A. with a little strut in my walk, a little cockiness in my talk. There was now an *official* balance of power.

Bunchy and I shook hands when I came back, and we buried any embryo of a grudge that could have developed right then. We began to work together closely again, although I must say that I never felt as completely trustful of Bunchy as I had before. (In fact, I have learned through a series of experiences—some not so pleasant—that to be completely open and trustful to any man or any woman is to invite them to step on you in some way.)

It was during the next few weeks, after I became Deputy Minister of Information, that I started political education classes in L.A. We would have these classes three times a week, and all ten section leaders were required to attend. They would be held responsible for conducting political education classes based on each week's lessons within their own sections.

Working together, L.A. and National Headquarters developed a standard format for these classes. George Murray, who was Minister of Education, would see that the chapters around the country more or less followed it, and would send out from National Headquarters, kits detailing the weekly lessons.

A unified political ideology on which everybody agrees is an absolute necessity in building a successful political Party. If there is agreement at the top, there is little problem gaining a consensus among the ranks. This is easily accomplished by a political indoctrination program. That the Party was able to do this was one of its initial secrets of success.

In L.A., the brother who assisted me in putting the political program into operation was John Jerome Huggins. In my estimation he was to develop into one of the most dedicated revolutionaries I have ever had the pleasure of knowing.

I had met John only a few months before when I had called our office to get somebody to come around to my apartment to give Kathleen Cleaver, Killer Wells (who had been staying with me), Bunchy and me a ride to the airport. John came around. Talking to him that day, I found him to be a very mature brother. I was immediately interested, seeing that he wasn't just a young brother off the block seeking excitement or who was getting his head whipped every day. It's a helluva thing to say, but it was easy to wonder why a brother with alternatives had chosen to get off into this type of thing, especially with the heat that was put on the Party.

John was from a middle-class Connecticut family, and had spent some time in the Navy. Not only did he come to give us that ride that day and assist in the political education classes, but day after day, month after month, I was to see him carry through every responsibility to the best of his ability, whatever might be the personal sacrifice involved.

John was very serious and softspoken. He had gone to college, but had dropped out, and had done some organizing around New Haven before he came to L.A. I think he told me Wendell Wade turned him on to the Party—they had known each other in the service.

One day, a brother named H.B. and I were sitting around my apartment listening to KBCA, an L.A. jazz station, when John dropped by. We were playing that game that brothers often do of trying to identify the cuts and the musicians before the DJ announces what was played, and who was playing (this is a game used to test your "hipness"). I remember John surprised me by knowing more of the cuts and sidemen than either H.B. or I, particularly if they dated back six months or more (I guess he hadn't much time to listen to the radio in the six months or so he had been in the Party).

The responsibilities did get larger for John—much larger than teaching a political education class—and he finally had to make the highest personal sacrifice—*his life*—when ambushed on January 17, 1969, at UCLA, allegedly by US gunmen.

Along with the thrice-weekly political education classes, we had begun to have weekly general meetings. They were held every Wednesday at 7 P.M., and usually lasted an hour or two. The main objective was to psychologically reinforce the membership, so that morale would not lag.

Bunchy, Banks, or I would speak. Every member in the L.A. chapter was required to attend. There were three hundred or more at the time, and each week there would be a couple of dozen newcomers.

As the speaker would be running it down, the hall would vibrate with enthusiastic cries of "right-on, right-on, right-on, brother!" At the end of the text for that week, the speaker would ask the newcomers if any wanted to come forward at the conclusion of the meeting and join the ranks of the Party.

It was at one of these meetings, a few weeks before our move out of the Black Congress into our our headquarters on Central Avenue, that we had another flare-up of trouble with US. The meeting was being held at the Black Congress.

It seems that just before the meeting started and before I arrived there myself, US had sent a group of Simba up to the Black Congress. One member of the top echelon of US confronted the highest ranking Party member who was there at the time and asked for an apology because a poster with a picture of their leader, Ron Karenga, had been defaced with slanderous remarks about the Maluana.

There was a heated exchange between the brother from the Party and the brother from US, but nothing much happened.

Later that night, Bunchy and I discussed the increasing friction between the Party and US in L.A. What was happening was that there was rampant name-calling and wolfing among the rank and file of the Party and US and the friction at that level was bringing about a situation that was becoming hard for the leadership to control.

We wanted peace. It would be impossible for us to ward off the police and have to worry about US at the same time. Bunchy and I decided to go to talk to Ron Karenga himself and see if we could call a halt to the bickering between our organizations.

The talks were arranged. Bunchy and I went to US central headquarters on Broadway one weekday night in the early part of June.

One of Karenga's men who had a clean-shaven head and was wearing a buba, both of which are trademarks of US, ushered us into Karenga's office. He was sitting behind his desk with one of his top lieutenants at his side.

The talks were not long. I doubt we were in there for more than thirty minutes. Both of us agreed that a war within the confines of the black community would not be to the advantage of either party. There was also some parrying back and forth concerning the relative strengths of our organizations.

Overall, it was a constructive meeting in that both parties agreed to issue orders to their ranks to stop the name-calling and bickering which was going on between them. (That was the last of the trouble with Ron Karenga's organization during my tour of duty in L.A. for the Party.)

Up north during this time the Peace and Freedom Party had entered a new arena with the candidacy of Eldridge for President on the PFP ticket (the idea had been conceived while he was in prison). This automatically made Eldridge the national titular head of that party, and put him in a position to call the shots within PFP, and to influence the direction of radical whites in what loomed as a pivotal year.

Also, PFP had given the Panthers a national base, physically through their campaign workers, and financially through campaign fund raisers. We were able to use this new mobility and the exposure which followed to move into binding relationships with the white radical movement, and at the same time go into the black communities across the country and organize Party chapters.

I think it was about this time that the agencies of law enforcement started a sustained drive to remove the Party from the scene. (Because of the peculiar racist attitudes of America, whenever black and white forces that declare themselves to the Left begin to work together, the Establishment pushes a panic button—even though, ironically, the coming together of black and white forces at any given time in the history of movements in America has signaled the containment and final destruction of those movements by internal difficulties even more than from external causes.)

There had been flurries of trouble before for the Party, but it seemed to me in July the pressure was really stepped up. The law enforcement agencies were probably very concerned about our promise of a classic retaliation if Huey was sent to the gas chamber. In all probability, they had also heavily infiltrated the organization, and could see that we were steadily building political influence and military might so that we had to be taken seriously (by July in L.A. we had over four hundred men and *were organized*).

The long arm of the law was beginning to move in many ways. For instance, at National Headquarters it was on the wire in the black communities of Oakland and San Francisco that anybody having information about Black Panther snipers could pick up some cash by giving this information to certain agencies.

Then there was the pressure that was beginning to be applied to individual members, in the hope that they would break. Bunchy would tell me of incidents where his parole officer was being obviously difficult. They began to try to find loopholes in Judge Sherwin's decision making Eldridge a free man, and they made an unsuccessful attempt to call him before the Adult Authority for a hearing. (This move, however, was nipped in the bud by a threat from Judge Sherwin that he would deem such action "contempt of court.")

The FBI began to bug me around this time on the pretext of investigating the bombing of my selective service draft board (I had been classified as 1A, and eligible for the draft, and I had protested, writing a letter to my draft board, letting them know that I was a black nationalist and dope addict, in that order.)

They came to my apartment and asked me to explain my whereabouts the night the draft board was blown up. After I had told them I would do the best I could, they tried to smoothly work into another line of questioning.

I remember on their first visit one of them asked me with a straight face if I was to hear of a riot starting, would I report it to them?

That was probably to establish whether or not I was the cooperative type.

I told them: "You must be crazy. I don't go for riots, but I'm not going to stop the brothers from expressing their disagreement with this country."

That stopped them momentarily, but I had to give them credit for being persistent. They would try to trick you into feeling at ease with them. In fact, the two FBI agents who visited me three times while I was in L.A. were so friendly that if we weren't in opposite camps, we probably would have struck up a very long conversation (when I went to New York, they must have transferred my dossier, for agents came around to friends of mine asking questions).

I also remember on that first visit, one of the agents asked me: "How did you happen to get involved with the Panthers?"

I shot back at him: "How did you happen to get involved with the FBI?"

I guess the shortness of my answers, the tone of my voice, and the look in my eyes (which must have conveyed my feelings that if I had any information "I would take it to my grave with me"), made them realize that they could better spend their time with other people. (Less than a year later, I would frequently read in the newspapers of "supposed" Party members who were "supposedly" giving up information to the law enforcement agencies. That is a tragic situation, to be seriously betrayed from within.) After three visits, they stopped calling on me.

After months of preliminary hearings, and a couple of continuations—Huey's trial opened on July 16, 1968. A week or two before the scheduled opening we had begun to organize a bus caravan of supporters to accompany the L.A. chapter membership on the trip to Oakland. We brought a couple of hundred people from L.A. to Oakland the weekend before the trial opened.

It was to be a lengthy trial, the final decision not coming down until September 9.

The Party had been waiting for this day, and on July 16 the final countdown before the showdown between the Party and the Oakland judicial, police, and administrative agencies began.

The day the trial opened we had over five thousand demonstrators in support of Huey lining the sidewalks in front of the Alameda Courthouse.

A group of Panther sisters, dressed in black skirts, sweaters, berets, leather jackets, and wearing Free Huey buttons, were positioned in front of the Courthouse at the entrance door. They were going through a rehearsed, rhythmic chant that went:
"Free Huey!
Black is Beautiful!
Set our warrior free!"

In front of the sisters, at either side of the door, two Panthers stood, holding a large powder blue flag with a picture of a leaping Black Panther—and the battle cry written on it: *Free Huey*.

Across the street from the Courthouse on the sidewalk in front of the small, very green park, there was a block-long line of Panthers, two deep. They were in uniform, and at a military rest position.

A mass of people, as many white as black, stood between the line of Panthers and the Courthouse. From the street you could clearly see at least fifty, blue-uniformed and silver-helmeted Oakland police, standing just inside the Court-house entrance. They rushed out once to maul Bob Avakian, the white PFP radical who was Eldridge's campaign manager, for tearing down the American flag from the Court-house flagpole.

Trouble was expected. You could sense that the TV people were avidly waiting for it. Huntley and Brinkley did a fifteen-minute special on their national show that day, which was pre-recorded and provocatively titled: "Two Armed Camps in Oakland: The Police and the Panthers." It showed the Party tailing the police with car radios keeping other Panthers posted as to what was happening, and it showed the police doing the same thing to the Party.

I think what blew everybody's minds that day, judging from the comments afterwards, was the control and discipline displayed by the Party. The stratagem for that day was: Be "cool," and don't react to the pigs. Act like they don't exist.

We had security teams with walkie-talkie radio sets patrolling the area in front and behind the Courthouse.

Their job was to make sure people were alerted if the pigs blew their cool. (In addition to the cops inside the Court-house, others were stationed on the rooftops in the surrounding area with high-powered rifles. A couple of blocks from the Courthouse there were paddy wagons and squad cars—ready.)

Since it was impossible to get into the courtroom (most of the seats were reserved for the press, and the tightest of security measures were being applied), we held a demonstration outside. A bus full of Party members would circle the Court-house, and using a bullhorn, a speaker would explain to the crowd the facts of Huey's case and just why the Party demanded his freedom.

Toward the close of the afternoon, Bobby Seale was standing atop the bus, speaking through the bullhorn when a motorcycle cop pulled alongside and called up to him, asking him to move on. This cop was treading dangerous ground, because he was sandwiched between the bus and the crowd outside the Courthouse entrance. The crowd started to close in on him, but Bobby warned the crowd to be cool, and he moved on. But for the tight discipline, this incident could have triggered a violent outburst, and when the motorcycle cop's reinforcements came in, a lot of innocent people could have been hurt, and it would have had no real connection to our showdown over Huey's fate. The bus circled the block, and within a few minutes came right back to the original spot. Bobby then continued talking.

For that entire week, we kept the ranks in Oakland and held disciplined demonstrations each day at the Alameda Courthouse. The countdown had finally begun.

|10|

The heat really begins to get bad in L.A. in August, and it is in that month that most of the action in L.A. has happened. As the temperature begins to climb, the toleration level of the black brothers and sisters seems to decline. (Watts kicked off in August '65.) August '68 promised to be an eventful August nationally, with Huey's trial going into its final days, and the Chicago political convention about to come off.

The Party had built a restless army in L.A., with no immediate war to fight. Since the beginning of Huey's trial two weeks before, it seemed that things would be controllable, that we could hold our army back. But Huey was convicted and sentenced to the gas chamber. We had anted up the game, and the stakes were very high: our lives against their lives if they made an attempt to take the life of Huey. We felt we could hold ourselves in check a little longer, but it was difficult in L.A., as I know it was in other chapters, because of the constant and steadily increasing surveillance and harassment by police, FBI, and CIA. They always seemed to be itching for the least little opportunity to provoke an incident with individuals, or the organization itself.

Despite this constant pressure in L.A., we restrained ourselves, although many times the effort left us totally frustrated, and nerve-racked. It seemed that we had learned to survive in an environment where enemies were constantly following us, lurking around corners, and making countless false accusations, all with the motive of intimidating us and making our lives as unpleasant as possible. We had adapted to this totally unfavorable situation in L.A., because it was to our advantage to do so at that time. We kept calm, while our enemies were frenzied around us, and for a while it seemed that our calm had succeeded in cooling the whole situation.

Monday, August 5, started as a routine day. I went to our headquarters on Central Avenue around noon. I checked with the sister at the front desk, who was taking care of the secretarial duties that day, for the calls and messages that had come in for me that morning. After taking care of the business around the office, I left word where I would be and went out to check with a section leader about the distribution of flyers announcing a Free Huey Rally.

When I returned to headquarters later that afternoon it was not any more crowded than usual, with about ten to fifteen people around. Whenever I was around the office and had time on my hands, I would go through a political education class with a small group of brothers. Today we gathered in a room to the rear of the front office, and began a discussion on a section of Mao Tse-tung's red book.

In the midst of our discussion the sister who was acting as secretary burst into the room. Her eyes were red and her voice was choked with emotion. "There's a report on the radio that the pigs have shot three brothers over on Adams near Crenshaw," she said.

There was a dead silence. The other brothers looked toward me. I was in charge and had the responsibility of deciding what to do. I knew we all had the same desperate thought—*After all, it might not be Panthers.*

"I'll check it out," I said.

I appointed a brother to carry on the class although I knew they would only go through the motions until the word had come back about who they were and what had happened. Then I asked one of the other brothers to accompany me, and we left the office to go to the scene of the shooting.

It took us about fifteen minutes to drive to Adams and Montclaire, which was where the shooting had occurred. We heard a report of the shooting on the car radio: Three black men had been shot and fatally wounded at a gas station shoot-out with the police. Two policemen had been seriously wounded, and the police were looking for a fourth man who had been with the three who were dead.

"Those goddamn pigs are at it again," I said to the brother riding with me.

"Yeah, there's probably going to be some shit," he replied.

Neither one of us dared to talk about the very real possibility that it was one of us. My skin seemed to tighten, my body felt warm and wet. The closer we came, the more I became engulfed in this feeling that it *had* to be one of us. Who else, I asked myself, what other people would be in a shoot-out where three of them were killed? One, yes. But *three* brothers, with their dick shot into the dirt? It could only happen to us.

I parked the car on Adams Boulevard. A block below us motorcycle cops had set up a roadblock, and it would have been too risky to chance being recognized. We took off our black leathers, and walked down the hill toward Montclaire, which intersects Adams Boulevard, one block from the main street of Crenshaw.

There were dozens of people around. They were standing in clusters, on either side of the street, from two blocks above the scene of the incident, where we had parked, down to the gas station where the shoot-out occurred.

I asked a few of the brothers what was happening. They told me what I already knew, that three black brothers had been shot and killed at the gas station below, and what I had reluctantly suspected, that they were believed to have been members of the Black Panther Party.

We walked down the hill to 11th Avenue, and crossed Adams Boulevard, to the gas station. There were cops everywhere. There were four squad cars in the filling station itself, along with a couple of cop motorcycles. TV camera crews in trucks were in the gas station; they had filmed for the dinnertime news the bodies of the three men who had been butchered in the gas station.

Large puddles of blood were still on the ground, but the bodies had been removed from the scene. Hovering above in the dusky sky were a couple of L.A. police helicopters.

After a few minutes we began to walk back to the car. An L.A. newsman, who frequently dropped around to the Party's headquarters, recognized us and rushed over.

"Do the Panthers want to make any statement about the killing of three of their members?" he said.

That validated what I had expected. He didn't realize that he had given me the information I had been searching for, but really didn't want to find.

"We'll make a statement when we find out more about what happened," I told him in an icy tone of voice.

We walked back up the hill toward the car. I saw a group of young brothers I recognized. I stopped and asked them if they knew what happened. One of the brothers there said that he had been across the street at Johnny's Pastrami Stand, and he had seen the shooting.

He said the brothers had pulled into the gas station, and parked at the gas pumps. The brother who was driving had gotten out and gone around to the front of the car and opened up the hood. The eyewitness said that a squad car had pulled up and that the cop who was driving went over to where the brother was standing with the hood of the car up. The second cop had gotten out and gone to the other side of the car. At this point things had happened fast, and the brother told me he was not certain, but it seemed that the second cop had opened fire on one of *our* brothers as he was getting out of the car. After that, the first opened fire, and it lasted only a few seconds. The brothers never really had a chance, although both of the cops were hit, and one brother had gotten away.

I thanked him for the information, and we continued to the car, and drove back to the office. We listened to reports of the shooting on the radio as we drove. They had more information now.

"One of the men has just died at General Receiving Hospital," the newscaster said. "He has been identified as Tommy Lewis, and was eighteen years old."

Little Tommy. I was enraged. I remember the words just machinegunned out of my mouth: "The motherfucking pigs have killed Little Tommy! The jive motherfuckers are going to pay for this!"

When we got back to headquarters, a two-block area around us was full of police squad cars, staked out. I know they were waiting for the word to move on our headquarters. There were a couple of squad cars right in the block where our office was located.

Inside the office, people were standing or sitting very still, nobody was saying anything. I knew that after the shock had worn off, they would be looking toward central staff to say *the word is go.*

One of the sisters had called around to the newspapers, and now we were able to complete the picture of what had happened. Steve Bartholomew had been driving, and was killed. Tommy Lewis and Robert Lawrence had been in the back and were both dead. Little Tony had gotten away (the police had said that all occupants of the car had weapons, and a couple of them were wearing bandoliers of bullets). Two cops had been wounded.

Steve would have been the ranking official in the group. He was the number-two captain in L.A. and always carried heavy responsibilities. Little Tommy was a lieutenant, and had come in with that first group of young brothers Bunchy had brought with him from the Teen Post (because of his youth and manner we felt for him in L.A. the same type of affection which was reserved for Little Bobby Hutton at National Headquarters.) Robert was also a lieutenant, and had joined the Party after he came out of the United States Marine Corps.

The phones at the office rang incessantly. Each call was important in its own way. One of the calls was to tell us that they had raided the house of Steve Bartholomew's girlfriend, and arrested one of our captains, Franko Diggs, and confiscated an arsenal of weapons. They had slapped an attempted murder charge on Franko.

With the cops all around us, it was clear that to function out of central headquarters would be impossible and we would be making ourselves a sitting target. Bunchy's house was only two blocks away, and still within their containment circle. It was decided that we would keep the office open as a decoy, but function mainly out of my apartment, which was on the westside in what is known as the apartment jungle. That night we set up our emergency headquarters there. Bunchy, Banks, a couple of Elite Squad, and a couple of top lieutenants stayed at the apartment constantly, going in and out to take care of necessary business. We had the place heavily armed, with a chopper (submachine gun), several high-powered rifles, and an assortment of pistols.

As the information continued to come to us that night, it was becoming clearer that the cops were planning a move against the Party. One clue was that the news media were always alluding to the Panther literature found on the dead men, but never saying that the police knew the men were Panthers. We knew that the police had confiscated Captain Steve's attache case, and it had all the names, addresses, and the organizational setup of the Party. I concluded that the only reason they had not made this public knowledge was that they wanted to prepare themselves to move with as little public attention as possible.

If they were going to try to come in and take us at the

apartment, we were ready to take it to the tape. We would have to make a stand right there for there was no place else to go.

We held meetings all that night, trying to regroup and get our intelligence in operation. We had to be able to counter any offensive the police made, or mount our own offensive if necessary. There was periodic telephone contact with National Headquarters to keep them posted.

We got word in that the fourth man, Steve Bartholomew's brother Little Tony, was safe. I didn't know where he was, but knew I could get in contact with him if necessary. That was good enough.

By the time day broke on the 6th, the police and FBI had the apartment staked out, as well as having headquarters completely surrounded. I had the feeling that we were in a vise, and they would start pressing at any moment.

Bunchy and I went to the *Free Press* that morning. They had some news for us. They told us that they had talked to one of Little Tony's relatives. She said that a policeman had called her and made a vicious threat against Little Tony's life. We gave them an interview for their paper which was coming out later that week.

There was a APB out for Little Tony, and his picture was spread all across the morning papers. I wanted him to go to Cuba (but it was not up to me, or any other Party member for that matter—it was up to Little Tony).

A group of conservative black leaders in the Black Congress had gotten together and according to their press conference, were talking with police chief Thomas Redding about arranging for the surrender of Little Tony, and convincing the Party not to provoke armed warfare with the police in the streets of L.A. It was true we were ready, but nowhere near as ready as the police, who would have had to be the ones to provoke an armed war.

These sycophants called my apartment, suggesting a deal. Our answer was a flat No. "No deals."

I decided to go on the radio that night with a special on the shoot-out, giving the Party's version. KPFK, an FM radio station with a large radical and liberal clientele had asked for an exclusive, and I said I would do it for the Party. If nothing else, I would tell thousands of people that the pigs had us jammed in, that we felt that they wanted to kill us, and that they were about to do that. If our prediction did come true, we wanted it to be broadcast throughout this country, that the L.A. police had been caught dirty, with the blood dripping from their fingers.

I went on the air at KPFK at seven o'clock that night of August 6. I had no notes, for I did not intend to make a speech, but I really unwound once I started. It was the Party's first public statement on the Battle of Montclaire, as it was to be called.

I explained that night the details of the shoot-out, which had finally been pieced together, mainly by people who were at the scene. I told how the brothers had gone into the gas station because their car was overheating and the driver, Steve Bartholomew, had gotten out and raised the hood. The two cops who had been following also got out of their car. One of them ordered Steve to open the trunk. The second cop ordered the brothers out of the car, and witnesses (by that time brothers who had seen it had called to give us all of the information), said they opened fire on Robert Lawrence, the first brother who got out. Steve rushed the first cop, having no choice but to defend himself, and was shot although not killed. Then Little Tommy came out of the back seat and was shot (no one knows whether he got off a shot himself (all the brothers were packing), nor is it known which cop shot him.)

Tommy did not die instantly, nor did Steve. It was reported that one of the cops walked up to Steve where he lay on the ground groaning in pain and agony and said: "Nigger, you should be dead . . . nigger," and shot him four or five times in the head. Little Tommy was on the ground clutching desperately for life, and they handcuffed him and kicked him in his wounds. He later succumbed at Central Receiving Hospital.

I explained how Governor Ronald Reagan (who was in Miami for the Republican Convention) had sent his Lieutenant Governor, Robert Finch, back to Los Angeles to explore "the potentially explosive racial situation" in the aftermath of the shooting. A conflict then developed, as Mayor Sam Yorty and Police Chief Thomas Redding said they could handle the situation. While all of these political hijinks were occurring, police intelligence had refused to divulge to the public the fact that this was another incident between the Party and the police, similar to ones which had been happening nationally, and that they had the Party members staked out.

Redding had made a statement a few weeks prior to the shooting, after Fred Ahmed Evans and his men had barbecued (killed) four pigs in Cleveland, that he had information that certain black nationalists in Los Angeles were heavily armed. I told the KPFK listeners that Redding's statement, the political maneuvering, the nondisclosure of information, and the fact that we had been garrisoned in, all pointed to the conclusion that the L.A. police were getting ready to murder as many of us as possible, and to make mass arrests. I assured the people that the Party would not de-escalate the struggle, and that in fact we considered ourselves in a *state of war* with the L.A. police.

I was still very wired up emotionally when I left the radio station that night. I don't ever remember being as angry in my life as I was those days right after the murder of the three brothers. I honestly felt like personally revenging the brothers' death, but common sense told me that if I didn't hang loose right then, they would probably have to make room for one more body.

I kept thinking to myself, as I was driving toward the apartment, about the ease with which Panthers were being killed, and I couldn't do anything about it, and nobody I knew could do anything about it. And I thought about the thousands upon thousands, reaching into the millions, of black people who have been murdered, and nobody could do anything about it.

What really burned me inside was that I was forced to realize the untenable position the Party and other blacks who dare to put their toe to the line are in. I knew that white people didn't really care that Little Tommy, Captain Steve, and Robert were gone, or that the pigs were scheming the murder of the rest of us. It was an alien world to most of them; their greatest involvement in the matter was watching the bodies carted away in front of their eyes, on their living room TV sets—the bridge between the international news and the sports on the dinner news. I had learned to accept that attitude from whites. But the painful reality was that many blacks also had it.

When you got down to it, we were pretty much alone. Not many people really cared, and I wished that night that I had the power to make them care.

I kept wondering when the day would come that a white man or a black traitor who took the life of one of our black youths would automatically know he owed us ten white lives to start, and that that was just a beginning and we were going to collect the debt immediately. If I could have asked Allah for one favor, that would have been it.

Three days passed.

The cops kept us staked out, but stayed a safe distance away. We stayed armed and ready. It was a Mexican standoff.

On Thursday, the fourth day after the Battle of Montclaire, the tension had eased somewhat. Bobby Seale and I spoke at noon that day to the TV and press and a large gathering of black people at the gas station where the brothers had been murdered. Our main message was that every black home should be well protected, and every black man and woman should be armed to the teeth.

That night I received a telephone call from the High

Command in Oakland, telling me that I was to pack and catch the earliest plane the next morning to San Francisco. I was going to Honolulu, Hawaii, in the morning, along with Kathleen Cleaver, then we were going to tour Japan together.

I was substituting for Eldridge, who was supposed to have gone to Hawaii with Kathleen, for the founding convention of the Peace and Freedom Party there, where he was to be nominated as the presidential candidate for that state. Then he and Kathleen had been invited to make a speaking tour of Japan, sponsored by *Beherein,* an organization of Japanese writers and artists. This tour was to coincide with a month of conferences in protest of the Vietnamese War and nuclear weapons. At the last minute, however, the parole board had slapped a travel bar on him.

I went to San Francisco the next morning, August 9. Eldridge met me at the airport and both of us went to the dining room there where we had a short meeting with Paul Jacobs, the writer and participant in radical causes, who was also a Peace and Freedom California senatorial candidate. After that, we left the airport and went back to Eldridge's house on Pine Street.

For the next hour or so, Eldridge and I talked about the situation in L.A. as it then stood, and the questions that might be raised on this international tour. It was to be the Party's first venture into the international arena, so what had to be accomplished politically was making the people of Japan (the Hawaii trip did not carry international import) see the parallelisms between our struggle, *and the way it is waged,* in the United States and other Third World struggles. This was made difficult by the tricky questions of land (are blacks fighting for land or separate states?), the transitional nature of black organizations, our earlier preoccupation with non-violence as our major ideological tenet, etc. There were no pat answers to these questions, but Eldridge felt the concerned people of Japan could be made to see that we were breaking new theoretical ground in the struggle of oppressed people around the world. The problems of the Third World are basically the same, only our strategy and tactics had to be different to fit the situation.*

Kathleen and I caught a United Airlines flight at about three that afternoon. The trip took us about five hours.

There was a good-sized delegation at the airport to meet us, and they carried signs saying *Welcome to Hawaii,* and threw leis around our necks. There were also several cops, standing right outside the delegation that greeted us, and keeping their eyes on us. Newspaper photographers kept asking us to pose for "just one more picture," and we gave a television interview on the spot.

We left the airport, and were taken to the home of the Joe Murphys', a very spacious, attractive house on top of one of the many hills of Hawaii. There was a cocktail party-reception in our honor, which was already in progress by the time we got there.

There were a handful of brothers at the reception (but no sisters). Since that trip I have traveled outside the country extensively and I have found that you can find brothers damn near anywhere—even Outer Mongolia probably has a few. Sometimes I'm tempted to say, "Brother, what the hell are you doing here, so far from the world?" The brothers at the reception introduced themselves. I remember a few of them: two roommates named Sleepy and Lewis, who both played basketball at the University, and Roy Walker, a brother from L.A. I became very close to Sleepy. He really had this thing for white women. He would defend to the bitter end their right to be included in any affairs of black men. During the speaking engagement that night I commented to

---

* Two weeks after Kathleen and I left, George Murray, Joudin Ford, and Landon Williams went to Cuba as political guests of the Cubans. All three of these brothers, who are very dedicated, are presently in jail, with the probability of being there a long time. Williams was accused of murder, in the alleged assassination of a supposed Panther who was actually a police informer.

Picking Up the Gun | 141

him that I didn't see the brothers in the audience with anything but Jezebels. Sleepy looked at me sideways, and said: "You don't approve of that." I told him: "I don't endorse it, although I try to understand." Sleepy smiled and said: "That's all I got." Sleepy came to L.A. in September, after I had completed the tour, and we spent a week or so together. I don't know whether he was trying to irk me, or he was serious, although I suspect the former, but he would make statements like: "This revolution is almost about freeing black men and white women." Sleepy had really got bitten by the bug.

After the reception, Kathleen and I were taken to the home of John and Mary Kelly, which was down by the beach. We were to be their house guests. I found the Kellys to be very fine people, and they made our stay very comfortable. But I laugh to myself when I think of John Kelly coming into his house and seeing Kathleen and me there for the first time. He came up and grabbed me by the hand, shook it firmly, and looked into my eyes. Then he did the same thing to Kathleen. Then turning to his wife, with uncontrolled enthusiasm he said, "Aren't they beautiful people." Meaning, of course, that black people in general are beautiful people, and here were two specimens before him to reaffirm the conclusion he had already arrived at—by what means, living in Hawaii, I don't know.

That night Kathleen and I spoke at McKinley Auditorium. There were over a thousand people who came, at two dollars a head, to hear us bring the word. At first the audience was inhibited, they weren't really with us. We had to work into it. Once you have spoken to enough audiences, you can more or less feel them out after a few minutes, and know how to best work on them. You might say it's like entertaining, except that you are carrying a social and political message.

After the audience warmed up to us, we really got off into it. The night was a success. Afterwards a bunch of us went over to a popular college hangout, The Gingerman, and then on over to the house of one of the brothers. We passed a pipe of hash, and when everybody was good and high, a discussion began that followed a pattern I've seen in every city that I've gone into, inside or outside the country, where there are over two brothers who hang together and want to meet you—they always want to hear your views of the black liberation struggle, but even more than that, each brother there wants to give *his* views.

The next day, Saturday, Kathleen and I were scheduled to leave in the evening for Japan. Kathleen spoke at the Peace and Freedom convention that afternoon, giving an acceptance speech for Eldridge. Then we rushed to the Japanese consulate to get our visas. They had told us on the phone that it would only be a matter of filling out a few forms, and would take less than an hour to complete.

When we got to the office around three o'clock, we were the only ones there. The consul came from behind his desk, gave us forms to fill out, and went back to his desk to read his afternoon newspaper. I was filling out a form when out of the corner of my eye I saw him look up from the newspaper at us, then back to the newspaper again, and then with an expression of disbelief look up at us again.

I knew what he had seen. The Honolulu afternoon newspaper—*The Honolulu Advertiser*—had a front-page six-column story about Kathleen and me speaking the night before, with individual pictures of us. I watched him quickly read the story, his face mirroring his increasing shock. I had read the story—it had quotes such as: "The United States is an international gangster;" and the general message about picking up the gun.

When we finished our forms and turned them over to him, he checked our names and I know the worst of his thoughts had been proven true. His hands trembled, as he read the names on the forms to himself.

Then he started the evasion act. It might take a little time, he said. He would have to wire his home office in Tokyo for an okay on our visas, since we could not be classified as tourists, or on business of a—and the next words seemed to have stuck in his throat for a second or so—"regular sort." Then we went through our own razzle-dazzle scene. Since it was obvious that he was going to put us uptight, we might as well be as difficult as possible. He was a quiet type of man, and it was easily seen that our complaints and accusations of imperialist-inspired deceit and unfairness caused him great discomfort and a certain amount of personal embarrassment. (I know he must have been happy nobody was in the office.)

He was sweating when he got back to his desk, but it did not hamper him from carrying through his mission, and tapping out a wire to his home office in Tokyo, and quoting the newspaper word for word. When he finished, he told us he would have an answer by that night, which was Saturday, and would contact us. But I knew that he was just trying to get us to leave the premises peacefully, and that it was going to be a problem getting into Japan.

That night he called to tell us he was having trouble getting a clearance on our visas to go to Japan. The next morning, the Honolulu newspaper, *The Bulletin*, carried the story of our being refused visas. (Our Peace and Freedom hosts had informed them.) We relaxed, and prepared to stay a few more days in Hawaii to see how things worked out, and then probably go home.

On Sunday, we placed a call to *Beherein* in Japan, telling them of our problem. *Beherein* promised to immediately organize a demonstration in front of the Japanese Foreign Ministry and the American Embassy, protesting the Japanese Government's refusal to grant us visas. They had thousands of people participating in the conference, which was in full swing. The demonstration took place Monday morning in Tokyo, which was Sunday by Hawaiian time. The next morning our visas were suddenly okayed. Kathleen had decided to go back to San Francisco, but I was going to continue on alone, carrying the word and seeing the world. I left that afternoon for Tokyo.

| 11 |

It was Monday night when I arrived in Tokyo. At the airport
I picked up an English edition of a Japanese newspaper and
they had a picture on the front page of the demonstration in
front of the Foreign Ministry. I learned later that none of
the other American delegations there, SNCC and SDS included, had encountered the problems that we had.

I was staying at the Hotel Dai Ichi, and the next morning,
John Wilson, the former deputy chairman of SNCC, whom
I had known very well in New York, also checked in. For
several weeks he had been touring the Japanese countryside.
I was happy to see John. That afternoon the Japanese radical students corralled John, Ken Cloak of SDS, and myself
and occupied our complete day and evening with political
discussions.

The radical Left student movement in Japan is very large.
The main grouping is called the Zengakuren, which is split
into numerous factions. There are the pro-Maoists, anti-
Maoists, Trotskyites, Stalinists, and countless others. During
my political tour of Japan, each of the factions in turn approached me, and asked me to speak to one of their caucuses,
or give an interview for their newspaper or magazine. The
sponsoring faction would always ask me leading questions

which were geared to bring a response from me that would be an ideological attack upon other Marxist-Leninist factions. (Sometimes they didn't bother to be sophisticated; at one interview in Tokyo, the Trotskyites attacked the Stalinists and asked me to agree with their attack just in principle.)

When John, Ken, and I were interviewed that night, I was asked one loaded question that was to recur time and again while I was in Japan (the same question had also been put countless times to SNCC's John Wilson and Donald Stone, which attested to the fact that it was considered very important by the Japanese left): "What about the reports that we are reading about the feuding between the Panthers and SNCC? (They were referring to the incident in July of that year when a group of Panthers had gone back to New York on a mission which was supposed to take us to the United Nations to present the facts of Huey's case and to demand a plebiscite. The UN visit had turned out to be unproductive, and so did the only other thing of importance that came out of that trip—a much publicized rumor of a split between SNCC and the Party which bordered on a shoot-out, and accusations that James Forman's life had been threatened. There had been no possibility of a shoot-out, and Forman's life was not threatened.) Although there was some truth in the rumors of disagreement, the actual incident had been blown completely out of proportion.

I answered this query by using the analogy of a family, with various members—brothers and sister, father and mother—composing the unit. I said that each member of the family had a different personality, and did things in a different way, and there would always be arguments of some sort within the family unit. One thing never changed—the fact that they were locked together as a family, closer to each other than to any outsider, and in general working together for the same ends. This family could only be damaged if it allowed an interloper to pry into its affairs, using its influence and power to champion the cause of one member against another, or magnifying an incident into major proportions—in effect, sitting in final judgment as to the right or wrong side of a disagreement or how important or unimportant it was. I was to use this explanation over and over again with many different groups.

I spoke to several caucuses of Japanese radical students my second day in Tokyo. Actually, the main action of the conference was taking place away from Tokyo, in the cities of the countryside, where each city would host the conference for two or three days. A body of thousands of people, Japanese and foreign delegates, was moving from city to city. My hosts, however, were still preparing my itinerary, since certain adjustments had to be made because of my belated arrival. I was scheduled to speak in Osaka on the fourth day.

I was looking at TV the night before I was to leave for Osaka, when *The Untouchables* came on the TV screen, in Japanese with English subtitles. I felt a sense of rage and helpless frustration to see a subtle thing like this which was so indicative of how the Western World has made people who are not like them, who do not share their experience, embrace their world, their thing, so completely. *I know that it was on this trip to Japan that for the first time I began to think about myself as a black man in the total context of what the Western World had done to me, and other people of color, politically, economically, culturally. The first taste of this new awareness was bitter, but it caused a personal renaissance within me, which saved me, I'm sure, from becoming a political degenerate, and I believe it will lead to my political salvation.*

I had *never* been committed to the political concept embraced by the Party that blacks and whites *should* and *could* integrate their efforts to work toward revolution in America. However, I had never openly opposed it. First, because it was Party policy to favor coalition efforts and, second, because I was subconsciously, I realize as I look back on it, taking a wait-and-see approach, knowing, of course, that I *might* be letting my emotions about this very fundamental political question dictate the way I acted. I was inclined to be highly emotional about the question of whether blacks and whites could work together in a revolutionary movement, and this was due to the fact that I could not shut out of my mind the reality of white inhumanity to blacks in the United States and the fact that white radical movements have never really attempted to change basic attitudes toward blacks among the white masses. (In America, such efforts by radical whites would indeed be revolutionary, and a lot of white radicals would probably get killed in the process.)

The first signs that let me know that my emotions had *not* betrayed me were the tactical pitfalls and entanglements I saw the Party fall into soon after beginning to work with white radicals—the most prominent example being the Peace and Freedom coalition. As soon as this coalition was entered into, the internal bickering and fratricide between the Party and other organizations in the black liberation movement heightened—almost in direct ratio to the involvement of radical whites. I remember how vividly this was demonstrated in the political races in the Bay Area, in which Panther candidates were running against other black political figures. Adding fuel to these political fires was the white radical press, which seemed to use every opportunity to make distinctions between the ideology, strategy, and tactics of the Panthers as opposed to those of other black organizations— most of whom were dubbed *cultural nationalists,* which has become a synonym for *reactionary.* It seemed that the white radicals were consciously building the image of the Party, and the price the Party was paying for these newly won allies was that it was becoming the enemy of other black organizations and political personalities.

In Japan, a nation of people of color, all of these things were replayed in my mind and came to me as I watched what was seemingly a harmless American TV program. This attempted Americanization or westernization of the Japanese people was only one step in a masterplan, for after the white man *westernizes* as many people of color as possible, around the world, they will become his bulwark against other people of color, who have not relented.

I thought to myself that night in Tokyo. This whole thing is like a giant stage, and the people of color are marionettes, and we are all being exploited and manipulated by the white man of the western world. And his self-assuredness in this role is the direct result of his feeling of racial superiority. And sadly, we the people of color are so naive at the game that we allow ourselves to become unwittingly used against each other. *This, I said to myself, is what is wrong with coalitions between blacks and whites in a revolutionary movement in America, whites are consciously or unconsciously pulling strings.* I remembered that with the Party, it seemed that once radical whites began to work with us, our complete political direction changed because of the anticipated response it caused in other black personalities and organizations—a response that seemed to keep the Party defending its actions a good deal of the time. This defensive attitude seemed to have led to a position where the white radical allies were defended at all costs, even if it brought the enmity of other black organizations and leaders. Once a political decision is made to uncompromisingly defend one's allies it naturally follows that you have also accepted their political reality, thereby giving these allies at the least a modicum of influence.

I asked myself whether the Party, being the recognized vanguard of the black liberation movement, would have been able to forge a united front of black organizations in America without the controversial alliances with white radicals? (I wanted to be honest, for the responsibility of a revolutionary is not to be popular in his analysis of a question but correct.) I still do not know the answer, although I do recognize that the alliances with white radicals served many immediate necessities for the Party. However, that night in Tokyo I made a personal decision that I was politically opposed to blacks and whites having an integrated struggle *at this time,* because the warranted suspicion by the black masses of the nature of the commitment of white people would make such integration of the struggle an impediment to mounting a mass movement of black people in this country. *And most important, I refused to be committed to a political strategy which would place me in the position of continuously reacting, and this is what seemed to happen to any black individual or organization that coalesced with the white radical movement.*

The next morning I left for Osaka, where I was to address the annual rally held in protest against nuclear weapons.

I was on the podium that night with about fifteen other speakers, from different movements and countries. Somebody told me that there were over ten thousand people in the audience, and as I glanced out over the stage lights at the sea of faces, I had to agree with that figure. As the other speakers took their turn, my interpreter and I went over my speech. At one point in the speech he wanted me to delete a reference to Mao Tse-tung, because he said it would offend the anti-Maoists in the audience. I did as he suggested.

I was the final speaker on the program, more or less the keynoter. Most of the thrust of the other speeches had been toward Marxist-Leninist interpretations of the speakers' various experiences and struggles, and the commendable, although somewhat romantic, cry to link arms in the mythical world revolution that was in progress. *I decided that my emphasis should be on another dimension of the struggle of third world people, the question of racism.* I opened as I always opened while speaking in Japan, by stating that our leader, Huey P. Newton, was a political prisoner and above all else my Party stated that he must be set free. Then I continued by outlining the two great problems that black people in America and people of color around the world are facing. The problems of *racism,* and *economic exploitation.*

When I brought up the question of racism, it automatically distinguished my articulation of revolutionary ideology as fundamentally different from what had been said before. I carefully explained that I was a socialist, and as such, by definition I believed that man's exploitation of man was for economic reasons, and the most advanced manifestation of this had taken the form of man's colonization of other men. But I added, and this was the cornerstone of my political philosophy, that this economic exploitation had taken a unique twist by justifying itself through propagating the myth that the white race was, and is, superior to people of color, and particularly black people. As is sometimes the case with aberrations, they magnify themselves, until they blot out everything that gave rise to them. *This I contended had been the case with racism, which is the greatest enemy of people of color and the greatest sin of the western world.*

As I argued my position that night, the applause was deafening. I do not mean to imply that there was unanimous support for what I said—that would be totally untrue—but I must have left some positive vibrations.

When I finished, and the program had been concluded, by all things, with the speakers linking arms across the stage, and leading the audience in the singing of *We Shall Overcome,* I went back to my hotel room.

My speech that night was the first articulation of my newly confirmed political belief that racism was *the* dominant problem for Afro-Americans, and a major one for other Third World people. It did not seem to me to be a glaring departure from the Party political line at *that* time, because the Party did recognize racism in America—although it always seemed unwilling to emphasize it in order to avoid being called racist in reverse. However, in the months to come, I became more and more firmly convinced that racism was the major obstacle facing Afro-Americans, and the political line of the Party openly put down emphasis on racism as being cultural nationalist and counterrevolutionary. (One of the main reasons I never brought my case before the High Command once I was suspended, was that I no longer embraced the political ideology of the Party, and I felt we would eventually have to go our separate ways, if for no other reason.)

A group of Japanese students came up to my room, seeking interviews for various university publications, and they introduced a line of questioning which I was to meet again when I was called on the carpet after I returned to Party headquarters (although the Party didn't bother to question —they corrected) and yet again in my later travels and political discussions with activists inside and outside the country, after my split with the Party. *The students failed to see racism as a major component of the problems facing people of color in the world.* I explained that their difficulty in understanding my emphasis on racism probably stemmed from the fact that they had never been victims of colonization; where because of the color of a man's skin his basic humanity is denied, and his culture, as well as his political and economic being, is not even made worthless, its existence is never recognized. I told them that I had directly and indirectly felt the weight of this colonization which manifests itself in racism, and the weight had been made heavy, almost unbearable, by the years of its presence, and I was no different in this way from so many black men, women, and children, wherever they might be in the world.

I recommended to these earnest Japanese students that they read the works of Dr. Fanon. I assured them that Dr. Fanon was a socialist, but first and foremost he was a colonized man, and for that reason I felt him more capable of speaking for my reality—or the reality of other blacks— than Karl Marx or V. I Lenin. (In March 1969, when I was a guest speaker before the African students at the Cité, in Paris, France, they argued vehemently for a strict interpretation of Marxist-Leninism, until fact after fact in our discussion intellectually, spiritually, and emotionally brought us back home. At the end of the evening, almost everybody was willing to admit that the white man had put something new in the game with racism, and that it was *our* problem to deal with it, and we had to come to grips with it before getting deep into Marxist dialectics.)

The next day, I spoke to a smaller group of conferences, and then left that evening for Okinawa. This would be the key speaking engagement of the tour, because Okinawa was a protectorate of the United States, as well as being her major nuclear airbase in the Near East, and the Okinawans had been fighting for many years to have Okinawa returned to their rule. I decided to make *Okinawa for the Okinawans* the thrust of my argument.

When I arrived on the island I was taken on a long trip by the customs people about my business there; they asked how long I would be staying, checked my bags, and put me through a lot of other little things nobody else in the line at the airport was bothered with. Finally, I was free to go, and with the two people who had come to the airport to meet me, I went to the hotel where I would be staying.

I was rooming with Don Stone of SNCC. Also at the hotel was Jim Harvey, a brother from Chicago, who headed a black cultural organization in that city. They warned me that the police security measures were tighter on this island than anywhere else they had been in Japan.

The next afternoon there was an outdoor rally near one of the airbases on the island. There were about ten speakers on the podium, with an audience of thousands of Japanese students sitting in the hot sun. (I cannot talk too much about the almost fanatical involvement of the radical Japanese students. Before my arrival, at one rally in northern Japan over one hundred thousand were in attendance. In America the only things that draw that attendance are pro football and Billy Graham.)

As each speaker took his turn, the applause and chanting gained fantastic momentum. I remarked to one of the brothers on stage: "These Japanese are like brothers, they might start to riot soon."

I received a tremendous ovation when I spoke. Particularly

when I lambasted the Japanese Prime Minister Sato as an "Uncle Tom," and Lyndon Johnson as an "international gangster." The police who had been lurking in the shade of the trees, just at the fringe of the crowd while the rally was going on, moved in right after the rally, and arrested hundreds of students. (They were charged with trespassing on government land, and deported to the mainlands, because after all, this was U.S. land.) We were hustled off and back to the hotel.

I stayed on the island of Okinawa two more days, speaking at various caucuses. Then I went back to Tokyo. I should say that there is so much interest in the black liberation movement in Japan that the presence of any one of the black brothers on the tour in any city warranted front-page news coverage, and not just in the radical Left newspapers, but even in the conservative newspapers.

In Tokyo I gave a series of interviews, mainly to present a clear picture of the legal case of my comrade Huey Newton. I was there two days, and then flew to Copenhagen, and from there to Prague, where there had been arrangements for me to speak to several radical groups.

I arrived in Prague a few days before the Russian tanks. Intrigue and suspense were heavy in the city, and my hosts advised me to cancel my speaking engagement and leave as soon as possible. I followed their advice, and caught a flight for Rome.

I was not going to do anything political in Rome, only rest a few days before I returned to American soil. I was physically, mentally, and emotionally exhausted from this brief but intense tour.

It was the last week of August '68, when I left Rome and went back to Los Angeles. The Battle of Chicago had been only a week or so before, and it was still on the lips of people. I think a lot of people really understood for the first time how cruel the police can be when they saw storm troopers savagely beating white radicals and even newsmen. Eldridge had gotten off into a verbal exchange with Governor Ronald Reagan, which started when he was appointed guest lecturer at the University of California. Reagan flipped his lid, and demanded that the University Regents rescind the appointment. Although they didn't give in completely, they made a desperate compromise, limiting Eldridge to one lecture instead of the originally planned ten.

On September 8, the decision came down on Huey. He was judged not guilty of first degree murder, but guilty of voluntary manslaughter. He was sentenced to two to fifteen years. I have to admit that in the beginning, a year before, I had thought Huey was destined for that cyanide pill, but miraculously we had made the Oakland Establishment back down. They had reached a *political solution,* one which had to be highly unfavorable to them. It was favorable to us, for I cannot see how the Party could have been successful in the only other alternative, a *military solution.* Still it was a hollow victory for Huey to have to spend two days behind bars, much less two years. Maybe the day will come, when black men will march into the courts with machine-guns and hand grenades, and free their comrades on the spot.

A week or so later, the California appellate court overturned Judge Sherwin's decision on Eldridge, and revoked Eldridge's parole. They gave him sixty days to get his affairs in order, and said that after that period—which was actually given him to allow him time to split—he was going back to prison.

Around the beginning of October I decided to pursue an interest I had always had, but never had time to develop due to my total involvement in the black liberation movement. I decided I wanted to write, and I wanted to write the story of the Panthers. I had been thinking about it for a while, but had held off until we were finished with Huey's trial.

This decision was not made in a vacuum. The story of the

Party needed to be told, and it is important for black activists to record their experiences, to serve as a guide for those who come after them. It was only because I believed this that I could make peace with myself about wanting to write, for I believe that individual skills and talents should serve some greater purpose than self-gratification or advancement, and maybe my writing would reach some receptive ears.

I went to New York in early October, and negotiated a contract to do a book on my experiences in the Black Panther Party with Dial. My intentions were honorable, and I felt it only fair that my comrades in the Black Panther Party who were more responsible than I in building the Party and its image, and therefore paved the way so that I could write such a book, should completely dictate how it should be written.

I went back to California with this in mind and contract in hand, thinking I would easily get the approval of the Central Committee. I never presented my case to the complete body, but certain very high members were totally opposed (and one person's arbitrary *no* shocked me, coming from him) to the whole idea. This high-handed attitude caught me completely off guard.

I must also say that the contents of my speeches in Japan, which dealt heavily with racism, had been severely criticized by a few very high officials in the Party (they had heard the tapes). I accepted their right to criticize, for the criticism was based on sound political logic—I believe it was somewhere around that time the Party was formulating its political ideology based on an analysis of society in terms of class exploitation—*but I did not accept this ideology.*

At that point, I had run afoul of certain members of the Central Committee on two counts: writing the book, and my political beliefs. However, things had not gotten bad, I guess they felt that with time I would submit to Party discipline, and they knew I did believe in the unity of the Party, and felt that no one person should assert his individuality over the Party's dictates. But on the other hand, there was something very arbitrary about a few members making decisions to which you had to submit without even being able to raise questions.

I had to do some thinking, for if the way I was feeling at that time—that I could no longer place my total life in the hands of the Party—was honest, I would have to leave the Party. I did not want to leave the Party, so I left my post in Los Angeles, went to New York, and hoped that I would have a change of heart.

In New York I was not politically active. I did make a trip to Montreal to a Black Writers' Conference, and to Nova Scotia with the Party's Prime Minister Stokely Carmichael. The only thing of political note that I did was in the latter part of October. I returned to Honolulu, with Stokely to fulfill a promise I had made to Sleepy that I would help get the Black Student Union at the University off the ground, by doing a couple of days of speaking. (We did help get them on their feet. We spoke to one audience of over eighteen thousand.)

I decided to go ahead and write the book. I could not accept a verdict which was arbitrary and never explained to me. I realized that my disobedience would put me in the bad graces of the Party, although I did not realize that would eventually cause an undying enmity on their part. (In their June 28, 1969 paper, the Party made countless vicious and untrue accusations against me, and closed the article by issuing their version of an All Points Bulletin requesting information about my whereabouts.)

Word came back to my agent's office in New York and the WBAI radio station (where I was scheduled to alternate with H. Rap Brown on a Friday night opinion show) that I had been silenced, and was under suspension. I accepted the suspension, the reasons having finally been decided upon: first, leaving my post in L.A., and second, the inability to submit to discipline.

In the latter part of November, I read, as did millions of other people, about the disappearance of Eldridge Cleaver, on the day he was scheduled to be returned to prison. I thought it a very smart move, and was not surprised. I never thought Eldridge would stand around and let the pigs make a sitting duck of him so that a few people who really don't give a damn would have another martyr to use for their own purposes. (Six months later, Eldridge was reported to be, and have been, living in Cuba. In July he showed up in Algeria for the opening of the first annual Pan-African Cultural Festival.)

On January 18, 1969, I read in the *New York Times* that Alprentice "Bunchy" Carter and John Jerome Huggins, (who had replaced me as Deputy Minister of Information) had been shot to death in a cafeteria at the University of California at Los Angeles. It was reported that the shooting, in which John and Bunchy never had a chance, was the result of a feud with a rival Los Angeles organization, Ron Karenga's US. (A few days later, the alleged gunmen, the Steiner brothers, reported to be US members, were picked up.) I was very deeply shocked at the deaths of John and Bunchy. I loved both of those brothers. For a few days I entertained thoughts of returning to the Party, but quickly quashed them because I instinctively knew that our problems had become magnified by time, and the pressures which were now on the Panthers.

I did not go to Bunchy's or John's funerals. I believe John's was a day in advance of Bunchy's, which made it the nineteenth Panther funeral, and was held in his home in Connecticut. Bunchy's was in L.A. They say he looked peaceful in the casket, and had a little red book clutched in the hand that was over his heart. Bunchy's brother Glen had had the first Panther funeral, and Bunchy's was the twentieth. (There were torrential rains in L.A. the day that Bunchy was buried, and it was reported that it rained steadily for twenty days and nights after that. I don't know if this meant anything. To some people I know it did, and I believe in signs.)

I went to Paris the first week in March. I was to finish writing my book in Europe, away from the thousands of things you can find to do in New York. I stayed in Paris with two young political activists, who have been active in Europe and Africa, M. and Mme. Herve. Mme. Herve is the former Julia Wright, daughter of the great author, Richard Wright.

Julia arranged for me to speak twice while I was there. Later I regretted this, since Chairman Bobby was to follow me into Paris. There were serious political ramifications, since people consciously or unconsciously distorted *what I clearly distinguished as my personal political views* as official or quasi-official.

While in Paris, I kept up with the activities of the Party by reading the Party newspaper. It was in March '69, that I first learned of the purge of the Party membership of people considered to be counterrevolutionary, opportunists, adventurists, etc. The purge had begun in February, right after Bunchy and John were shot, and I surmised that the shock of having two top officials gunned down had spurred the Party to start tightening ranks. Each week in the Panther paper, names of people purged were listed. I recognized many as top officials, deeply involved in Panther activities. I was surprised that people of this caliber had been purged.

In the early part of April '69, I went to Stockholm, where I actually completed the book. Regrettably my arrival in Stockholm followed Chairman Bobby's which had followed Stokely's. (I was to see Bobby on Swedish TV criticizing Stokely's political line, and saying that he would be reprimanded once he got back to Central Committee. Stokely later resigned in July '69, saying the Party's practices were "coercive and dishonest.") This created a peculiar type of confusion, which I tried my best to alleviate by saying to anyone who asked: "I am not here for political reasons. I will not comment officially on the Black Panther Party. I am here to write." I did write a few essays for magazines, expressing my views on the black liberation struggle.

I think it despicable that interlopers continue to play

black personalities and leaders against each other. I think it unfortunate that black personalities, or leaders (those who actually command people), allow themselves to be used, pimped, in this way. I refer to the white Left who are always pitting black personalities against each other, ideologically, and to the mass media which uses any differences between personalities to create a situation of drama and melodrama for the public. *I firmly believe that this is what set the stage for Malcolm X to be assassinated.*

It was in the latter part of April, when one of the brothers in Stockholm brought me a copy of the March 29, 1969, Panther newspaper which officially confirmed what I had already suspected—*that I had been expelled from the Party*—and as one of my enemies (he had become my enemy by his own admission because I was out of grace with the High Command) said to one of my friends: *"Barred for life, in disgrace."*